The Care & Feeding

of a

Dancer

By Toni Tickel Branner, MA
and Jenna Lee Branner, Dancer

Care & Feeding of a Dancer

Published by Blue Water Press
Waxhaw, North Carolina

First Printing September 2007
Library of Congress Control Number: 2007935843
ISBN: 978-0-9796046-0-7

Cover design – Frank Rivera
Cover Photography – Jeff Carvotta, Carvotta Photography
Peter Noble, Universal Events Photography
Illustrations – Frank Foster
Interior design and layout – 1106 Design

Printed in Canada.

A book cannot replace personal guidance from a physician, registered
dietitian, or trained exercise professional. The advice in this book
includes general information based on research and is not designed to
treat any specific disease or condition.

When dealing with the pressures of training and competition, it is important to know there are many variables that affect performance, such as genetics, development, and emotional maturity. Yet nutrition is a major component that is too often overlooked for its benefits of providing energy and chemical protection for optimal performance.

—Paul Stricker, MD, FAAP, Sports Medicine Pediatrician and Olympic Physician, From his book Sports Success Rx!

Table of Contents

Foreword

By Paul R. Stricker, MD
Sports Medicine Pediatrician and Olympic Physician
Author of *Sports Success Rx!—Your Child's Prescription for the Best Experience*

As a sports medicine pediatrician, I have found that many young athletes are eager to learn about their sport, improve their technique, find the best coach, and have the newest equipment to help their performance. Many of them utilize all of these tools and achieve some benefit. Many of them realize they need something more. Something profound. Those who understand the value of good nutrition often hit the jackpot since the body can have all the training tools in the world, but be unable to perform without excellent nutrients to supply the body's exercise demands.

I was honored when Toni Branner asked me to contribute the Foreword to her *The Care & Feeding of a Dancer*. Her personal experience, knowledge, and commitment to the health of young people is exemplary, and an example of supporting our children's health without compromise. The information she provides should be used as tools upon which to build a great framework of performance benefits. Although the secret of whole food nutrition is not rocket science, its simplicity is also not a quick fix. Sound nutritional habits for the family will not only provide for the current exercise and school needs, but also provide for the long term health and well-being of your children.

Years ago, it was known how carbohydrates provide useful energy for exercise. Later, science taught us the vital importance of replenishing carbohydrate stores quickly after intense exercise. More recently, research has exposed another important aspect of exercise and sports performance we must control—oxidative stress. Being able to neutralize harmful chemicals produced with exercise and emotional stress is accomplished with the powerful nutrients in fruits and vegetables. Mothers have been telling us this for years, but now we know a lot more about why certain foods offer so much to the long term health of our bodies.

Toni's books offer much more than nutritional help, and emphasize that nutrition is just part of the overall picture. Fluids are immensely important, and a well-hydrated athlete is ready for optimal performance. Physical training, adequate rest, and emotional stamina are aspects that are required. Supporting your child without pressure is critical, and I appreciate the many aspects of the sports experience that are covered in these pages. Understanding all of the factors that go into sports activities is the first step to a successful outcome.

Approaching sports and exercise as a family is a great analogy to the "team" on which your young athletes participate. You ARE all in this together! Everyone can contribute to better health of the family, whether everyone is involved in dance or not. So be a team player and enjoy what reading lies ahead.

Toni Branner changed my life. It is amazing how spending forty-five minutes with Toni can have such an impact on how you fuel and take care of your body. Her sessions with dancers, children, young adults, and parents can lay the groundwork for healthy bodies and prevention of major health issues. Toni's passion, drive, knowledge, and enthusiasm for health are contagious, and I am so proud to have her as a friend and colleague.

—Gary Pate,
Dance Teacher, Owner and Director of Starpower Dance Competitions and WILD Dance Conventions

Dancing has become my life and my profession. I received my degree in elementary education and was all set to teach, but dance kept pulling me back. It's in my blood and is the reason I am who I am today. There are so many avenues of dance besides performing. So don't get discouraged if those auditions aren't going according to plan. Keep trying and know that there is something out there for you. Cherish every minute of being able to dance. It's a gift—it teaches self-confidence, stamina, dedication, and you know you are doing something positive for your health and body. Never give up!

—Noelle Pate Inman, Director, Power Pak, WILD Dance Intensive, Assistant Director, Starpower Dance Competition, Dancer, Singer

Acknowledgements

I would like to thank the advisors and contributors who helped us with this book. I would first like to thank my husband, Billy, who with a little training from Jenna has become the model dance dad. I would also like to thank younger brother, Will, who took the "If you can't beat them—join them" attitude, and now travels with the dance team as part of the hip-hop squad while doing sports on the side. My mother, Becky Brown, who taught me about nutrition and the importance of muscle balance and core strength, many years before they were studied by personal trainers and dance instructors. Dr. Paul Stricker, whose passion for helping young athletes and their parents is an inspiration for all of us who care about the future of children.

Thank you to the many incredible teachers and dancers who offered encouragement, support, and the opportunity to allow us to get this information to young dancers. Allyson Weir, Nina Schulte, Caroline Lewis, Gary Pate, and Pam Chancey, are a few who should be recognized for their effort and dedication to nutrition and the "Care of the Dancer."

Thank you, too, to the health professionals who have the courage to teach the truth regarding disease prevention and the achievement of optimal health. Just choosing the small fries instead of the large is not enough. Although a plant-based diet may seem strange, it is not as hard as it seems. The research is very clear, and even very young dancers can understand concepts like oxidative stress and free radical damage.

Thank you to Jeff Cravotta and Peter Noble for the amazing cover photography. Both gentlemen really understand how to capture the joy of dance in photographs. Finally, I would like to thank my co-author Jenna. Having you as a daughter is even better than I ever imagined. You are smart and talented and always kind to others. I can highly recommend her as a role model for your dancer.

—Sincerely,
Toni Tickel Branner, MA
Exercise Physiologist and Wellness Consultant

Board of Advisors and Contributors

Charee Boulter, PhD
Charee Boulter is a Licensed Psychologist specializing in eating disorders, performance enhancement, substance abuse prevention, stress management, and mindfulness meditation.

William A. Branner, III, MD
Physician, Dance Dad, Contributor.

Tina Marie Mendieta, MS, RD/LDN
Registered dietitian, dancer, fitness instructor, and wellness consultant.

Pam Popper, PhD, ND
Naturopathic Physician, Nutritionist, Owner of The Wellness Forum.

Paul Stricker, MD, FAAP
Sports Medicine Pediatrician and Olympic Physician
Author of *Sports Success Rx!—Your Child's Prescription for the Best Experience.*

The most important advice I could give a dancer is to be confident and love yourself. To dance is the most raw and intimate form of art. Every day we put ourselves out there, only to be criticized and broken down. It is not easy, but what in life is? Trusting yourself and your talent is essential to success. It is easy to give up and quit, however, it is not easy to look back and wish you had pushed harder or continued with your passion.

—Caroline Lewis
Professional Dancer, Choreographer, Teacher

Introduction

This book came to be for several reasons. In my twenty years as an exercise physiologist, I have spent many hours teaching and training coaches, athletes, corporate executives, senior citizens, and others who want to improve performance and prevent disease. As I attended dance competitions with my daughter, I started noticing how hard these children were working but how poorly they were taking care of themselves. Dancers are athletes in the truest sense of the word. They train for hours in the studio and push themselves to high levels during performances. They deserve the same attention and education in regard to nutrition, muscle care, and sports psychology as the elite athletes receive.

As a dance family we have also learned much about how to make this huge financial and time commitment to dance work for us in a positive way. Sharing these tips and techniques, as well as mistakes we have made along the way, may save you some trouble and propel your family forward to a beneficial and fun experience. Dancers, please share the family chapter with your Mom, Dad and younger brother or sister. The sooner you recruit them to your dance support team, the more fun and enjoyment you all will experience.

This book is for all types of dancers but especially those who would like to move up to the next level. Ballet dancers, competition dancers, or "I'm doing this just for fun" dancers will all benefit from the practical advice and strategies. It doesn't matter if you plan or hope to be a professional dancer. All of the advice in this book will help you grow up to be a healthy and successful adult. Although I never danced after high school, I was able to accomplish many things in my life because of the skills I gained as a dancer. First and foremost, I know how to organize my time and juggle many projects at once. This is exactly what I had to do with school, chores, and dance class when I was a student. I was a college cheerleader and was able to travel around the country and the world with the University of North Carolina Chapel Hill teams. Because of dance, I can easily count music and lead an aerobics class. This paid my way through graduate school. I then became the owner of my own company and a professional speaker. I have no problem standing in front of hundreds of people to teach a seminar. I owe this to the confidence and performance experience I gained through dance.

What makes the information in The Care & Feeding series of books different? The nutrition and physical training guidelines are based on state-of-the-art-research. You want to be healthy now and improve performance, but the approach in this book leads you into a lifetime of optimal health. We are just now coming to understand how important a plant-based diet is to current and long-term health and disease prevention. Starting a dancer on this road at a young age means they will deal with less illness, less disease, and fewer problems with weight control than the generation before them. Other topics like reducing dairy consumption, consuming less animal protein, and consuming the recommended daily phytonutrients are concepts that are incorporated into the suggestions for healthy eating. Injury prevention by proper warm-up and physical training are often neglected areas of education for the dancer and are explained in these pages. The challenge for dancers and parents is to utilize the recommended resources to continue to learn about wellness and discuss these topics as a family.

You, the dancer, are the inspiration for *The Care & Feeding of a Dancer*. So, plop down on the floor in your center split and start reading.

Dancers, take care of your bodies. Respect yourself and know that this is the only body your get. Be aware of what and when you eat and drink tons of water. Close friends of mine have been affected by eating disorders and I can only say that an eating disorder will control and ruin your life. Don't let yourself get sucked into that lifestyle. Believe me, it's no life at all. Keep your body strong, happy, and healthy. Love yourself and help each other. Keep dancing and stay healthy!

—Adrienne Renee Canterna
Professional Dancer, Complexions and Universal Ballet,
Choreographer, Director: American Dance Artists

1. The Love of Dance

—with Jenna Lee Branner

It is important to be passionate about something in your life. If that something is dancing then you have found an eternal obsession that will remain a part of your life for as long as you live. But how do you know you really LOVE to dance? The answer to this question is not to be decided by your parents or anyone but yourself. It will hit you one day—probably when you are lying on your studio's floor, sweating, hurting, about to pass out, but still loving every minute of it—that you really love to dance. Or perhaps you will realize it when you are overcome with emotion in the middle of a lyrical class and you have no idea why.

It doesn't matter what your reason for dancing. There are dancers of all sizes, ages, genders, and personalities all doing the same thing. Whether you are dancing for fun, dancing to stay in shape, or dancing to make a career out of it, you are a dancer and you share a common bond with other dancers. I have friends from all over the country that I have met through dance. I go to conventions and intensives on weekends and in the summer to exciting cities and fun places. I have travelled to Italy to take classes from teachers from many other countries. It is so nice to stay in touch with people who have the same drive and focus that I do. Dancers have a unique ability to have fun no matter how dire the circumstances. We have been freezing at an outdoor set waiting to shoot a music video, staying up until 1:00 in the morning at an extra-long dance competition, and surviving the toughest and most critical teachers and choreographers. Sometimes a choreographer will lose track of time when they are creating a dance piece. I once went 8 hours without anything to eat and without leaving the dance room. Dancers develop a higher tolerance for fatigue and pain. When the football players at school complain about their aches and bruises I can honestly relate. Dance truly prepares you for real life.

Joining a dance company or a competition team is a big decision that you should make with the help of your parents.

When I was a little girl I woke up every morning asking my mom, "When do I dance today?" Being a part of a company is for dancers who are not content with just one recital every year. We want to be on the stage every chance we can get. If your goal is winning competitions you might be competing for the wrong reason. Judging in dance is very subjective so one day a ballet dancer might win and another day a hip-hop dancer comes in first. As long as you are doing it for the love of performing then every competition will be a success. The judges' decision is not a reflection on you but it is just their opinion on that particular day.

> Dance is a passion that only other dancers will understand. Cherish every moment.
>
> —Jeremy Hudson, Professional Dancer, Teacher, Choreographer

I don't think I could do what I do at school and at dance class without taking care of my body and health through good nutrition and muscle care. I have learned that it takes a lot of planning to do as much as I do without getting run down and sick. I pack snacks for my dance bag and a cooler of water before school. I don't mind when the kids at school tease me about how different my lunch looks compared to their pizza and fries. Some of them have tried and liked new, healthier foods because of me. Just a simple thing like making sure you are hydrated will improve your dance and your performance at school. You don't get a new body when you get older so now is your chance to learn about healthy eating, warming up, and stress management.

As a dancer, you learn how to push yourself to your fullest potential and to take criticism as well as compliments. You feel pain, you experience success, you deal with defeat, and you gain irreplaceable friendships with other dancers. You have something to fall back on when everything else in your life is going wrong. If you truly love to dance, it will never leave you. Even if your body fails you one day, you will dance in your mind and soul.

Yes, It hurts!

—Terry Beemer
Dancer, Aerialist, Choreographer,
Teacher of Dance and Circus Performance

The Main Pointe

With hard work, a positive attitude, good training, and the right nutrition, you can rise to your fullest potential as a dancer, but you have to love it first.

2. How to Choose a Dance Studio

One of the most important decisions a family makes is the choice of a dance studio or dance company. If you live in a smaller town you may not have a choice but for many, there are at least several options available in their city. The right choice for your next-door neighbor may not be the best choice for you. Your goals may change as you get older, so you might need to switch studios or someday you might move and have to research your options.

Here are some questions to ask yourself before you begin:

- Do I want to focus on just ballet and pointe or do I want to include tap, jazz, and contemporary training?

- How far away am I willing to travel to take class?

- Do I want to dance year round with extra performances or just take class and do one recital each year?

- Do I want to exercise and have fun or do I want to strive for a high level of dance technique and ability?

- How much money can my family afford to spend on my dance training, costumes, and travel?

Many studios will allow you to come and take a few classes or at least observe to get a feel for the atmosphere. Here are some points to consider:

Philosophy of the Studio

Do the classes seem tense or is there an atmosphere of nurturing, discipline, and gentle control? Do they offer a competition company? A ballet company? Recital classes only? What styles of dance are offered? Are technique classes offered year round? What performance opportunities are offered? Are they affiliated with any professional companies? Does the studio bring in guest teachers or regularly attend dance conventions? Does the studio participate in community service activities?

Qualifications of Teachers

What training and experience do the teachers have? It is not critical that teachers have former professional dance experience but they should have a wide and varied background of training. Do they have a basic knowledge of first aid and anatomy and physiology? Do they participate in continuing education opportunities for dance teachers? Are the teachers willing to meet with parents to answer questions and meet with the dancer? Do the teachers seem professional and organized? Are the teachers good role models for the students?

Environment

Is the studio in a safe location? Is the parking lot well lit?

Does it seem clean and inviting inside? Is there a place for dancers to change, have a snack, and relax between classes? A warm temperature is best for working muscles. A wooden floor that is raised (or sprung) is best for cushioning landings. It can be covered by a marley floor, which is a vinyl or linoleum material that allows for better traction and control. Are there windows that allow for observation of the students by parents and visitors? If not, do they have a schedule that allows parents to observe on a regular basis? Are the music selections appropriate and well organized?

Auditions and Dancer Qualifications

How are auditions held for various levels at this studio? Are students grouped by their age, by their ability, or both? Are there any weight limits or emphasis on body type? You want a strong focus on healthy nutrition and body image but not an obsession with thin dancers. Are educational programs on nutrition, body image, and muscle care offered to the students?

Support for Advanced and Serious Students

Are there older, more advanced students to serve as role models? What is the typical class size for each age group? Are there alumni from the school who are now dancing or teaching professionally? Are there regular ballet and technique classes year round? Are master classes offered so students are exposed to a variety of dance and choreography styles? Does the studio offer trips to study in other cities? Do they offer help for students in preparing for auditions for summer intensives and other programs?

Finances

Competition dancing is very expensive. Ask for a full, written statement of tuition for classes, estimates for costumes, and extra expenses like conventions and entry fees for competitions. Many studios have fundraising opportunities to defray the cost so ask about this as well.

A dance teacher is so much more than just an instructor passing along their knowledge and passion—they are mothers, friends, therapists, costume designers, set design specialists—the list goes on and on.

—Allyson Weir, Director, Weir Dancin' in Charlotte, NC, Choreographer, Costume Designer, Competition Judge

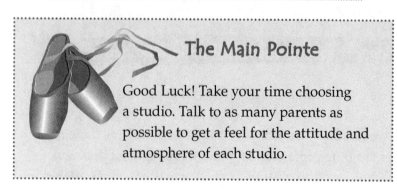

The Main Pointe

Good Luck! Take your time choosing a studio. Talk to as many parents as possible to get a feel for the attitude and atmosphere of each studio.

3. Developing the Total Dancer

It was once thought that dancers did not need training outside of regular barre work, technique and practice with various choreography styles. Traditional teachers felt that physical training outside of traditional dance could hurt artistic expression. Some were worried that activities like weight training and Pilates could be detrimental to the dancer's form and range of motion but this has proven to be untrue. Today, the world of dance is so physical and competitive that it is now expected that dancers train for endurance, power, strength, and flexibility just like any other athlete. This method, called "cross-training," is proven to improve performance in all sports. Prevention of injuries and muscle balance are two of the best reasons to add strength training, core exercises, and focused flexibility to the dancer's regimen. Many famous athletes like football player Herschel Walker, diver Greg Louganis, and martial arts expert Bruce Lee used ballet training to improve their performance in their sport. Dancers can take the many training techniques that athletes use to move up the ladder to the next level.

Nothing will be handed to you. You gotta learn how to hustle. You have to put your time in.

—Roman Vasquez
Professional Dancer, Choreographer, Teacher

Let's take a look at the various components of a "fit" dancer:

Cardiovascular Endurance (Aerobic Fitness)

The word aerobic means "with oxygen." Oxygen is necessary to burn the fuels which produce energy for prolonged activity. By exercising aerobically, we initiate physiologic changes which increase the efficiency of the heart, lungs, and circulatory system. A healthy heart has the ability to supply plenty of oxygen and nutrients to the working muscles during normal activities and dance movement, as well as any emergency situations which might arise. During a 10-hour competition or rehearsal, it is important for your last performance to be as great as your first. Dancers with aerobic endurance will not fatigue at the end of a long production routine or at the end of a demanding day of classes.

Aerobic activities are those that are rhythmical, continuous, and involve large muscle groups. Aerobic activities such as walking, running, cycling, swimming, and aerobic dance increase the heart rate to a target level and maintain it at that level for a certain length of time. Some dance programs incorporate aerobic conditioning into their classes and some do not. You may need to add in your own aerobic conditioning or consult with a personal trainer if you need to supplement your dance classes. In order to get a training effect, you must do regular aerobic activity. It does not help to do a nice jog every couple of weeks. Two-to-three workouts a week for 30 to 45 minutes are the minimum to maintain aerobic conditioning. Sometimes this is all you have time for and that's OK. During off-weeks, during the summer or on vacation, you could add a few more days. If you are trying to lose weight, going for extra walks or jogs will make a difference. Your dance teacher might run dances back-to-back for 20 to 30 minutes with no rest. This can be very effective, specific aerobic training.

Special Note: With any high-impact activities like running, jumping rope, or aerobic dance you should wear well-fitted, supportive shoes. Dancers have enough wear and tear on their feet without going for a jog or jumping repetitively in bare feet.

Develop Muscular Strength and Endurance

Muscular strength is the amount of force a muscle can exert or resist for a brief period of time. Research and practical experience tell us that if we stress a muscle or muscle group more than it is normally used to, it will eventually adapt and improve its function. Therefore, certain exercises are designed to increase strength so that we may perform our everyday activities with less exertion and less chance of injury. New research tells us that muscular strengthening exercises play a key part in preventing osteoporosis and decreases in metabolism. If a muscle is stressed less than it is usually accustomed to, it will atrophy and lose strength. Broken limbs are good examples. The limb is immobilized for a length of time and when the cast is removed, one limb is usually smaller than the other. The same thing happens when you neglect strength training. When your muscle mass is decreased you will experience a decreased resting metabolism and less strength in your dance moves.

If I can teach anything to my kids that I teach, it is to take care of their bodies. To feed and strengthen what God gave us to work with is vital to success. I see a lack of overall mental and physical strength in kids today and it saddens me. They are not conditioned like they should be. We are athletes and therefore must care for our bodies in that manner.

—Caroline Lewis, Professional Dancer, Certified Personal Trainer, Faculty for Shock Dance Convention and The Southern Strutt Dance Company

Professionals now agree that strength training can be an essential part of a complete dance program. Care must be taken to develop long, lean muscles with power in a way that does not decrease flexibility and range of movement in the joints.

Muscular endurance describes the ability of muscles to sustain repeated contractions or apply sustained force against a fixed object. If having muscular strength allows you to lift your dance partner, then having muscular endurance allows you to lift her 20 times during one rehearsal. Activities such as ballet class, jazz technique exercises, sit-ups, push-ups, raking leaves, shoveling snow, and pushing a lawn mower all require prolonged muscular exertion. Safe and effective muscle training can be accomplished in dance class or on your own with the help of a trainer.

Exercises utilizing weight training, calisthenics, and rubber bands will help to increase muscular strength and endurance. A lighter weight with more repetitions is best for dancers. Usually, three sets of 15 to 25 repetitions of each muscle exercise will accomplish this goal. Variety is important, so switching routines every couple of weeks will keep dancers from reaching a plateau in development. Circuit training actually works well in a studio setting and it is easy to change the stations often.

Muscular Balance

One of the most common reasons that dancers experience injury is due to muscle strength and flexibility in the joints becoming out-of-balance. Most dancers compensate for weakness or add to the imbalance by using one side more than the other, or their "good" side is featured in the choreography so they end up overusing one side of a muscle group. Often individuals have sufficient strength in some muscle groups but are deficient in others. For example, we use our quadriceps (thigh muscles) every time we kick, walk, run, climb stairs, etc. Our hamstrings (back of the thigh) usually receive no significant exercise during everyday activities. The stronger quadriceps pull with more force on the skeletal system, especially the hip, back, and knee. This kind of muscular imbalance is often the source of lower back pain, hip pain, knee injuries, and various other injuries. It can also affect your posture, movement patterns, and make you more prone to injuries from other reasons. Thus, when using strength training you must concentrate on these weaker muscles to create balance.

A good rule to remember is: stretch the strong muscles and strengthen the weak ones. If you have time, work on all of them.

Extra Strengthening for These Muscle Groups:

• Rectus abdominis, transverse abdominis, and internal and external obliques (abs)

• Erector spinae (lower back)

• Hamstrings (back of thigh)

- Abductor (outer thigh)

- Rhomboids (upper back)

- Deltoids (top of shoulders)

- Triceps (back of upper arm)

Include these muscle groups if you have time and add extra stretching:

- Iliopsoas (hip flexors, front of hips)

- Quadriceps (front of thigh)

- Adductors (inner thigh)

- Gastrocnemius (calf muscles)

- Biceps (upper arm)

Functional Strength and Core Stabilization

Exercises that help prepare you for real-life activities require functional training. By recreating the movement patterns you use in your daily activities you become stronger and more prepared for work and recreation. Your mom or dad may only need enough fitness to mow the grass and bring in the groceries but a dancer needs a much higher level to perform successfully without injury.

Focusing on coordination, balance, muscular control, and the speed of movements are some ways to work on functional fitness. Mimicking the actual movement when you exercise is a simple way to accomplish this. An example would be practicing the motions of picking up your dance partner but with a weight instead of the actual dancer. Dancers use a lot of abdominal core strength and oblique strength as they turn and twist in the air. You can train for this by incorporating twisting and side crunches into a strength program. It is also important to evaluate how much flexibility is necessary for your specific activities and to train with that goal in mind.

Your core muscles include your abdominal muscles, your back muscles and smaller muscles involved in posture and support of the spine. Dancers should include exercises that focus on keeping the core muscles stable and strong as well as increasing strength during movement. Stability balls and standing exercises are great for improving core strength. Functional training should only be used in conjunction with traditional strength training.

Flexibility

Flexibility is the range of motion possible around a joint. Stretching exercises are utilized to maintain or increase this range of movement, to help prevent muscle soreness, and to prevent long-term injuries. This is one of the most important components of fitness for the dancer. Some dancers are naturally very flexible and others have to work much harder to obtain an adequate level.

Then come the lights shining on you from above.
You are a performer. You forget all you learned,
the process of technique, the fear, pain, you even
forget who you are. You become one with the music,
the lights, indeed one with the dance.

—Shirley MacLaine

Studies have shown that stretching is most effective when performed at the end of the aerobic or muscular workout when the muscles are warm all the way to the core. For dancers, it is necessary to stretch gently in the beginning of class after the circulatory warm up but the more intense stretching should be at the end of class or after a long period of intense movement.

Since flexibility is specific to every joint, it is incorrect to refer to flexibility in a general sense, e.g., "Katie has good flexibility." Each joint must be evaluated separately. Another common misconception is to assume that to have good flexibility, a person must have an excessive amount. There are some dancers who are so flexible that it is difficult for them to control movement or they are very injury-prone. Dancers and athletes often place their bodies in positions which stretch muscles and connective tissue beyond the point deemed necessary for normal function. They do this to maximize performance and to achieve artistic effects but this is why dancers require special coaching and conditioning in order to avoid injuries. A well-trained dance teacher or personal trainer will be able to gradually help you to improve and maintain your flexibility level for all joints.

Body Composition

Your body weight includes the weight of all your muscles, bones, organs, body fluids, and body fat. If the fat is removed, all that remains is your lean body mass. Too much adipose tissue (fat) has been associated with many health risks including heart disease, diabetes, hypertension, arthritis, gall bladder disease, cirrhosis of the liver, hernia, intestinal problems, and sleep disorders. Exercises like dancing work to increase the lean body mass and decrease body fat.

Your percentage of body fat is a much better indicator of your fitness than your weight. For example, many athletes, including dancers, would be overweight according to typical weight charts. However, if we measured their percentage of body fat, it would probably be low or within normal ranges. There are also many thin, sedentary people who weigh very little but have a high percentage of body fat. For example, a person with whom I'm working, and who smokes, is 5'6" but only weighs 113 pounds. Her body fat is 32%, which is in the obese range. It would be dangerous for her to lose weight—she must exercise to increase her lean muscle mass. Do not become discouraged if you weigh more than your friends who do not dance. Chances are that your lean muscle mass just makes you weigh a little heavier on the scales.

> The mirror is not you.
> The mirror is you looking at yourself.
>
> —George Balanchine

Long-term regular exercise usually decreases body fat but does not always have an immediate effect on body weight. This is because you are gaining muscle mass as you lose the fat. If you are trying to lose excess weight, do not become discouraged if your weight does not change immediately. Remember that your body composition is improving. If you can imagine the fat cells in your body just hanging out, not needing much (fuel, oxygen, etc.), not doing much—just there. Now picture your muscle cells—constantly using energy, needing huge deliveries of oxygen, and staying very busy. Because lean (muscle) tissue is more metabolically active than fat, you will burn more calories all of the time, even when you are sitting around or sleeping. Exercise also increases your ability to mobilize and oxidize fat. This enhances weight-loss efforts, conserving lean body mass and preventing the regaining of lost body fat. If you are dancing a lot and still feel like you need to decrease fat and increase muscle, you might need to focus on the food you are eating. The right exercise and optimal diet are both necessary to achieve optimal body composition.

Body fat varies widely even between fit individuals. We do know that the average person in the United States tends to be overly fat. Women are considered to be obese at a body fat of 32% or higher, men at 25% or higher. Women are considered to be fit at 21 to 24% body-fat and men at 14–17%. Dancers and gymnasts are usually in the 12 to 18% category. Females who drop below 10 to 13% may cease menstruating. This decreased estrogen level promotes calcium loss from the bones, increasing the risk of fractures and osteoporosis. This is a common problem for those with eating disorders, long distance runners, and other extreme endurance athletes. As a dancer, if you stop menstruating for more than three months, make sure you consult your doctor. It could be that you are training too hard and/or not eating enough calories.

The Main Pointe

Understanding the components of fitness will help you know how to train to improve those you need for excelling in dance.

4. Let's Get Warm!

D ancers often make the mistake of equating the words "warm-up" and "stretching." They are not the same. They comprise two separate parts of your pre-dance routine. Most dancers walk into the studio and plop down into a big straddle sit and start to stretch as they await the start of class. Although stretching exercises should be included before class, as part of class, and before a performance, the most important goal is to increase the core body temperature and to prepare the muscles, connective tissue, and circulatory system to safely accommodate more intense movement. Stretching "cold" can be more harmful than not stretching at all. A proper warm-up improves performance, allows you to focus, and reduces the chance of injury and muscle soreness.

The warm-up is divided into three parts:

The Circulatory or Thermal Warm-up

The circulatory warm up should be designed to raise your core body temperature and the local temperature of muscles, ligaments, and tendons. It should also increase blood flow to the working muscles and increase your rate of breathing. It involves continuous, rhythmic, full-body movement like walking, marching, light jogging, prancing, or hopping.

"Marking" a dance could also work as a circulatory warm-up. Improved blood flow will bring oxygen and nutrients to your cells and waste products can be removed. Your energy systems are activated to provide more fuel for your muscles and your heart rate increases to accommodate the upcoming strenuous movement. The higher body temperature allows nervous impulses to travel faster which maximizes coordination. In your muscle, the mechanical efficiency of contraction is enhanced, so your muscle contractions can be quicker and more forceful. Synovial fluid is released into your joints to lubricate, reduce friction, and promote smooth and more comfortable movement.

> To dance is to be out of yourself, larger, more beautiful, more powerful. This is power, it is glory on earth and it is yours for the taking.
>
> —Agnes De Mille

This warm-up might only last 5 or 10 minutes in a warm studio or could take 10 to 15 minutes in a cold environment. Remember that *no stretching* should be included during this segment. The circulatory warm-up should continue until a light perspiration is present. At this point you should not feel tired or out of breath. Your heart rate and breathing are slightly elevated, your muscles are warmer, and you are ready to begin range of motion warm-ups.

Advanced dancers often need a longer warm-up than beginners. The more in-shape you are and the harder you train, the longer it takes to achieve the same effects from your warm-up.

The Range of Motion Warm-up

The movement in this section is designed to lubricate your joints and prepare them for more intense activity. You should mimic patterns and paths that your body will soon be required to perform. Bend and straighten knees (plies) and elbows. Roll your ankles, wrists, shoulders, and torso. Move your body front to back, side to side, and up and down. This is usually included as part of your ballet barre work or technique class. If you are attending a rehearsal or performance you may need to arrive early do this on your own.

The Stretching Warm-up

Now you are warm, your muscles are more elastic and your tendons, ligaments, and other connective tissues are ready to lengthen and stretch. Warm tissues stretch more easily, providing more permanent results and less risk of injury. Equal stretching of each joint will improve your posture and body symmetry, increase range of motion, delay the onset of muscle fatigue, and minimize soreness. Never violently force a stretch. Notice signs that you may be overextending your limits. There is a difference between the discomfort of stretching and actual pain. Some dancers are naturally very flexible and others have to spend much time on this part of their training. If you are trying to improve your flexibility you might need to warm-up and spend time stretching on your own.

Types of Stretching

Ballistic stretching consists of quick, repetitive, bouncing-type movements. The momentum can result in damage to muscle and connective tissue and may be responsible for increased muscle soreness. This is not the best method for beginning dancers or for recovery of injuries. In special circumstances, however, this method may help advanced dancers prepare for challenging and vigorous choreography.

Static Stretching involves gradually going into a position of stretch until tension is felt. The position is then held for 10 to 30 seconds or even longer. Since static stretching is more controlled, there is less chance of exceeding the limits of the tissue, thereby creating injury. Research shows that after six seconds, a stretch reflex kicks in and allows the muscle to relax. This is why after you hold a position for a while you can then stretch a little farther.

Dynamic stretching involves moving slowly and with control through a range of motion. You must have completed a thermal warm-up for this to be safe. An example of a dynamic stretch would be a standing calf stretch with the heel flat on the floor. Now slowly bend the knee, lift the heel and press the heel back to the floor. Repeat 4 times.

Contract-and-Relax methods involve contraction of muscles or muscle groups for 5 to 10 seconds followed by relaxing and stretching with extra pressure. Traditionally, this procedure has been utilized by physical therapists but can be used very successfully with dancers. Use this method with caution, as some of the positions require a partner, which increases the risk of overstretching and consequent injury.

Active Isolated Flexibility is performed with a rope and involves contracting a muscle to relax the targeted muscle in preparation of its stretch. This is a very effective technique but requires proper instruction. Visit Michele Assaf's class at Broadway Dance Center in New York City or purchase her video.

The Main Pointe

Warming up and stretching are not the same thing. Warm-up to increase your core body temperature and blood flow, increase energy production, improve coordination, and prevent muscle injury. Stretch only after you are warm and sweating slightly.

Dancing requires an incredible amount of stamina. In order to produce specific movements, our bodies must use many muscles all at once. Therefore, it is absolutely vital that one has the fuel one needs for maximum performance and to stay healthy and avoid injury. When our bodies are weak they tend to compensate and work through it, creating a huge risk for strain and injury.

—Courtney Connor
Dancer, Cincinnati Ballet

5. Advanced Performance Training

Interval Training

Interval training is a powerful technique for dancers and for people who just want to improve their fitness and promote weight loss. Most of your performances and competitions require bursts of energy for 1 to 4 minutes, followed by complete rest, and then this is repeated. Interval training is simply alternating bursts of intense activity with intervals of lighter activity during your classes or training sessions. During intense exercise, muscles produce the waste product lactic acid. Too much lactic acid can make exercise painful and exhausting. By alternating bursts of intense exercise with easier intervals, you'll help reduce the buildup of lactic acid in your muscles. Your body will become more efficient at moving the lactic acid out between routines and your next routine will be stronger.

If you want to do interval training on your own, start with walking. If you're in good shape, you might incorporate short bursts of jogging into your regular brisk walks. If you're less fit, you might alternate leisurely walking with periods of faster walking. For example, if you're walking outdoors, you could walk faster between certain mailboxes, trees or other landmarks. There is no set length or intensity for the intervals; it is up to your dance instructor, your personal trainer, or you. The only rule is that you have to complete a circulatory warm-up before you begin.

Benefits of Interval Training

You'll burn more calories. The more vigorously you exercise, the more calories you'll burn—even if you increase intensity for just a few minutes at a time.

You'll improve your aerobic capacity. As your cardiovascular fitness improves, you'll be able to exercise longer or with more intensity.

It adds variety and reduces boredom. Turning up your intensity in short intervals can add variety to your exercise routine.

You don't need special equipment. You can simply modify your current routine.

Safety Precautions for Interval Training

Even trained dancers should start slowly when utilizing a new exercise plan. If you rush into a strenuous workout before your body is ready, you may hurt your muscles, tendons or bones. Instead, start slowly. Try just one or two higher intensity intervals during each workout at first. If you think you're overdoing it, slow down. As your stamina improves, challenge yourself to vary the pace. You may be surprised by the results.

Muscular Strength and Endurance

Muscular strength is the force you can apply by using your muscles. Muscular endurance is usually measured by counting the number of times you can perform a movement before fatigue sets in. Both fitness goals can usually be accomplished by resistance training which may include: calisthenics using your own body weight (push-ups), weight training with machines, free weights, or resistance bands.

The following prescription should be used by dancers to increase overall strength, endurance and muscle balance: focus more on strength, increase the weight and decrease the repetitions. Focus more on endurance, decrease the weight and increase the repetitions. The American College of Sports Medicine recommends training at least two non-consecutive days per week, although three days would allow faster progress. Some athletes do weight training every day but alternate muscle groups. An example would be: on Mon/Wed/Fri—work on arms, chest, and back, and then on Tue/Thur/Sat—work on legs and abs. These suggestions all depend on your fitness level and the time available. Most dancers benefit by doing a well-rounded program of 8 to 12 repetitions or 10 muscle groups 2 to 3 days per week.

General Guidelines

Sets: perform 1 to 3 sets with weights or bands. Three sets are optimal especially during the pre-season or off-season for dance. You can maintain your strength gains with one set once the season starts.

Repetitions: begin at 8 repetitions, and work up to 12. This gives you the best mix of strength and endurance. When 12 are easy, increase the weight slightly and go back to 8 repetitions. This way you will continue to increase strength and endurance.

Weight or Resistance: choose a weight so that you feel the fatigue on the last 3 to 4 repetitions. Young dancers under 14 should stick with fairly light weights and do more repetitions. Exercise bands work great in the dance studio and do not require much space to store.

Vary Your Workout: every few weeks or months, change your workout slightly so you will continue to improve. You can change the type of exercise, the number of repetitions, the speed of the contraction, etc.

Safety Tips for Strength Training

Never perform muscle work without completing a circulatory warm-up.

Only lift weights with an adult present or a qualified spotter.

Utilize proper form and body position. If any position or exercise causes discomfort it should be discontinued immediately. The back and the knee are most vulnerable to injury, so avoid locking the knee and never hyperextend (arch) the lower back while lifting weights.

Slower is better for beginners. Once you have a base of strength and general fitness you can learn to train more for power. Many high-level athletes use too much momentum when weight training. Try doing super slow reps for some of your workouts. New studies show significant increases in strength with this method.

When performing standing exercises, bend your knees. This is called the "neutral pelvic position" and keeps your spine in the best position to support weight and movement.

Circuit Training

Circuit training is designed to combine cardiovascular training with strength, endurance, power and agility moves. You can do this on your own, with a trainer, or in the dance studio with the rest of your team. Set up a series of exercises in a circle. I usually use 6 to 12 stations depending on how many dancers are going to participate and my goal for training them that day. Alternate the aerobic stations with strength and power moves. You can use timed stations or a set number of repetitions. Start each dancer at a different station. One benefit to this method is that you can work every muscle group and keep your heart rate up during the entire workout. You can make your circuits very specific to your goals.

Sample circuit for dancers who want to improve leaps and jumps: Do each station continuously for one minute.

Station One: Jump rope

Station Two: Jump squats with toes to the front

Station Three: Walking lunges with shoulder press (weighted ball)

Station Four: Push-ups (on knees for beginners) or bench press

Station Five: Plyometric jumps onto a box

Station Six: Sideways gallop pulling feet together (in the air) in the center of the movement (30 seconds on each side—can be done on a treadmill with incline)

Station Seven: Abdominal crunches

Station Eight: Up-Up Down-Down footwork drill, on and off a step. 30 seconds—lead with right, then 30 seconds—lead with left

Station Nine: Pull downs for the upper back (with weights or bands)

Station Ten: Jump squats (toes turned out)

Station Eleven: Torso circle with weighted ball for core muscles—30 seconds right/30 seconds left

Station Twelve: Triceps dips on weight machine, box, or a bench

Start over and repeat for a total of three circuits.

Plyometrics: Training for Power

Plyometrics is a method of training for and developing explosive power. Dancers may not call it plyometrics but much of their training already utilizes these concepts in class and in performance. We know that the concept of progressive overload (working muscles harder than they are normally accustomed to working) builds strength, endurance, and power. By performing exercises and movements that emphasize strength, speed, and agility and then taking them to the point of overload, a dancer should see an improvement in specific skills like leaping, kicking, jumping, and lifting. If you choose to add plyometrics, enlist a certified athletic personal trainer to help you develop a program. Safety is very important because you will be working at a very high intensity. Techniques for jumping, landing, foot placement, and posture are crucial for success. The principle of specificity is very important in plyometrics. Specificity means concentrating on a specific or particular individual muscle or group of muscles in exactly the same way it will be used in the dance movement. Training that mimics the same angles and contractions that you will be using in your performance will also improve neuromuscular skills.

You will experience more muscle soreness with this intense kind of training. The breakdown of muscle tissue and recovery is part of the process of increasing power, so a day of rest between workouts is usually required. Research has shown that young athletes will see improvement with 2 to 3 training sessions per week.

Other Specific Training Techniques for Dancers

Active-Isolated Strength and Flexibility Programs
These training systems are designed to pinpoint, isolate and strengthen individual muscles. Developed by Jim (exercise physiologist) and Phil (sports therapist) Wharton and adapted for dancers by Michele Assaf at the Broadway Dance

Center, these methods reduce your workload by removing tightness, so that you can swing your limbs more freely. These stretches transport oxygen to sore muscles and quickly remove toxins from muscles, so recovery is faster for dancers and athletes of all levels. Most of the exercises are practiced with a rope, towel, or light weight with each exercise designed to work or stretch a specific muscle group. I love the attention to the ankles, feet, and toes in this program. The best way to learn these techniques is to attend a class or learn from a video (see Recommended Resources).

Pilates

Pilates or Physical mind method, is a series of non-impact exercises designed by Joseph Pilates to develop strength, flexibility, balance, and inner awareness. This method strengthens and lengthens muscles without causing bulk which is perfect for dancers. Posture, core strength, balance, and circulation will all be improved. Dancers are often able to do advanced level Pilates after first learning basic techniques. The best way to incorporate Pilates into your training is to take a class from a certified instructor or work from a video.

Yoga

The term *yoga* comes from a Sanskrit word which means yoke or union. Yoga postures are used to tone, strengthen and align the body. These postures are performed to make the spine supple and healthy and to promote blood flow to all the organs, glands, and tissues, keeping all the bodily systems healthy. Mentally, yoga uses breathing techniques and meditation to quiet and discipline the mind. Dancers benefit from yoga in many ways. It is a great time to focus on the mind-body connection and to develop better health and fitness in general. A qualified instructor is crucial to making sure your yoga postures are performed with proper technique. Yoga is often used when a dancer is rehabilitating an injury.

Tapering: The Power of Rest

Most dancers train year round and have many times during the year when they need to hit a "peak performance." Tapering is a training technique designed to reverse the fatigue that occurs during heavy training, without losing any training benefits that you have worked so hard to achieve. It is the final phase of training prior to important competitions,

and involves a reduction in training load by lowering training intensity, frequency, and duration.

The word "peaking" is also used in the same way as tapering. The period of time required for an optimal taper will vary depending on the dancer and the time available between competitions or performances. A taper period that is too long in duration or reduces training volume too rapidly may not provide sufficient training stimulus to prevent losing what you have gained. A taper period that is too short or fails to reduce training volume sufficiently will not allow enough time for full physiological and mental recovery.

Benefits of an Effective Taper:

• More glycogen in the leg muscles (this also depends on proper dietary intake)

• Increased density of red blood cells

• Increased blood plasma

• Increased enzyme activity in the leg muscles

• Increased size of muscle fibers (increased strength and power)

• Increased maximal oxygen uptake (better aerobic ability)

• Improvement in the neural system (coordination, reaction time, and agility)

Taper periods range from 4 to 28 days. For dance, shorter tapers are usually necessary because of competitions and performances that are within weeks or days of each other. Different age groups within a dance studio may require different taper plans. The younger dancers may perform on Friday and the older dancers on Sunday. Research has shown that tapering produces improvements in performance of 1% to 22%.

A less technical approach to tapering would be to simply pay attention to your sleep habits and your ability to rest between training sessions, classes, and performances. When things get too busy and intense, your body will respond with more sickness and signs of over-training. One of the best skills to develop as a young dancer is the ability to listen to your body.

The Main Pointe

Dancers are artists and athletes. Your performance should look effortless, but in order for your body to be the best creative instrument, it must first be trained to maximize all of the components of fitness. Power, speed, strength, agility, and flexibility are just as important as skill, artistry, and style development.

6. Injury Prevention and Treatment

Dancers occasionally have to deal with chronic and acute injuries. Dancers usually have a high pain tolerance and sometimes let small injuries go until they become more bothersome and chronic. Teachers should spend a substantial amount of time on muscle balance, flexibility, posture, and alignment because excessive tension on joints is the most common cause of injuries. Learning to listen carefully to what your body is telling you is a crucial dancer skill. Look for patterns in how your body feels. You might want to keep a journal of which movements cause discomfort or pain. Are you favoring one side over the other? This will help a sports medicine professional diagnose more quickly and accurately. Prevention is always best, but when injuries do occur you have to adjust your dance schedule and recognize and treat the problem.

Daily Checklist for Dancer Injury Prevention, Safety, and Health:

- Am I hydrated?

- Have I eaten a small meal recently to provide energy for this activity?

• Check the dance surface for pins, sharp objects or loose parts on props.

• Do I have the proper shoes for this type of class or performance?

• Have I performed a circulatory warm-up to prepare my joints?

• Am I focused and ready to concentrate?

The PRICE Treatment for Dance Injuries

Several things happen when ice is applied to injured tissue. The blood vessels constrict, decreasing blood flow to the area. This reduces bleeding and therefore, swelling. Cold also acts as an anesthetic, controlling pain and relieving muscle spasms. Ice slows down metabolism around the injury slowing the release of histamine that increases inflammation and swelling. You can use ice packs, ice baths, or ice massages. Apply as quickly as possible.

PROTECTION: Protect the area from additional injury.

REST: Stop immediately when you feel pain.

ICE: Apply ice for 20 to 30 minutes several times per day. Try a frozen bag of peas in a thin cloth.

COMPRESSION: Firmly wrap the injured area (not too tightly) with elastic or compression bandages. Bandages should reach from the largest area below the injury up to the largest area above the injury.

ELEVATION: Raise the affected area level with or slightly above the heart to encourage blood flow to and from the injury.

Heat should never be applied too soon or it will increase swelling and bleeding into tissues. Wait at least 72 hours after the injury before applying heat (warm, not hot) to increase blood flow to the area. This will increase blood flow and oxygen to the area and remove accumulated waste products. Apply 2 to 3 times a day for 20 to 30 minutes at a time. After two or three days, you can alternate cold with heat (contrast bath)—hot for 1 to 2 minutes (96 to 98 degrees) and then cold (55 to 64 degrees) for 1 to 2 minutes. Repeat several times and finish with cold for 5 minutes. In all cases, if pain becomes worse or persists for a prolonged period, seek medical attention immediately. Proceed slowly upon resuming your activity.

Common Injuries Associated with Exercise

Muscle Soreness (Delayed Onset Muscle Soreness)
Breakdown and repair of muscle tissue results in stronger muscle, therefore, mild muscle soreness may be a good

sign. Muscle soreness usually occurs when you begin a new exercise regimen, perform eccentric contractions (lengthening the muscle), or change your normal training routine. Attending a convention or a class from a guest teacher will challenge your body in different ways and cause soreness. Microscopic tears in the muscle or connective tissue may require several days of rest for tissue repair and rebuilding. Severe soreness is unnecessary. The key is prevention. Progress slowly. Start with a low number of repetitions and low intensity, and make sure you warm up and cool-down properly. Avoid ballistic movements and stretches. If you do become sore, it will usually last 24 to 48 hours regardless of what you do to treat it. Sometimes repeating mild exercise the following day and then performing slow, static stretches will relieve some of the discomfort. Massage and warm baths may also help.

> Dance like it's the last time you will ever dance again. Be fearless—take risks—dance out of your comfort zone. You have to look bad before you look good.
>
> —Mark Meismer, Professional Dancer, Teacher, Choreographer

Foot Injuries

Your most used "instruments" in dance are attached to each of your legs. Taking care of your feet is one of the most commonly overlooked aspects of dance training. Common complaints that affect dancers include rubbing shoes, tired, aching feet and foot pain. Dancers who dance without shoes or with foot thongs probably need calluses and tougher skin. If you go to get a pedicure do not let them rub off your rough skin. Your feet need it for protection. Start with professional fitting of your pointe, tap, and other shoes. Buy the correct padding and learn how to use it properly. Other common foot problems are blisters, corns and calluses, athlete's foot, heel pain, over-pronation, and sesamoiditis. Blisters should not be broken. Let them dry out. Try moleskin cut into a donut shape to protect the blister. See Recommended Resources for Web sites that will help you treat foot problems.

Shin Splints

Inflammation or pain occurring where the muscles and tendons attach to bones can cause pain in the front portion of the lower leg. This can result from dancing barefoot, or in poorly fitted shoes. It can also be caused from an improper practice surface or from a program which is too intense. An imbalance between the gastrocnemius and the tibialis anterior may also contribute to shin problems. Other causes of shin splints include: a lowered arch (flat feet), decreased flexibility in the Achilles tendon, irritated membranes, tearing of muscle where it attaches to bone, hairline or stress fracture of the bone, or other factors. The best treatment is the PRICE treatment, however, stopping the aggravating activity and switching to a low impact activity for a while may allow time for healing while maintaining fitness. See a medical doctor to rule out fractures.

Helpful Hint: Ask your teacher if you can wear supportive sneakers to Technique and Leaps and Turns class until your injury heals. This gives the foot and leg more cushioning and arch support.

Knee Problems

Pain in the knee can be very difficult to diagnose. Many times it is the result of overuse, poorly fitted shoes, improper surfaces, or biomechanical problems. Using a proper progression, avoiding uneven surfaces, making sure your muscles are balanced, and not allowing injuries to become chronic will help prevent serious knee problems. Always see a physician and physical therapist if pain persists.

Ankle Problems

Ankle sprains are the most common ankle injury. Prevention includes strengthening exercises, adequate warm-up, proper footwear and ankle bracing. Activities that require quick changes of direction or exercises performed on an uneven surface may increase the chance of sprains. If an ankle injury should occur, the ankle should be iced immediately and medical treatment should be sought.

Helpful Hint: If you are dancing in and around props, be very careful as this is a common way for ankle sprains and breaks to occur.

Achilles Tendon

Achilles tendonitis, which is inflammation of the sheath around the Achilles tendon, can cause severe pain and is a frequent complaint of dancers and distance runners. Usually, improper shoes and lack of flexibility are the culprits. Stretching, or ice and rest are the best treatment.

> I do not try to dance better than anyone else. I only try to dance better than myself.
>
> —Mikhail Baryshnikov

Side Stitch
This is a sharp pain in the side beneath the ribs. Possible causes for this pain include: an oxygen deficiency, gas pains, spasms of the diaphragm, or an improper warm-up. Often it will disappear if you: lower the intensity of your activity, take slow, deep breaths, or bend toward the stitch and press gently on the painful area. Make sure you are not eating too large of a meal or a meal too high in fat or sugar before you dance, as this will cause cramping.

Heat Injuries
In extremely hot temperatures or high humidity you need to be very careful to avoid heat cramps, heat exhaustion, and heat stroke. Heat cramps are the mildest form of heat-related injuries. Symptoms include muscle twitches and cramping in the arms, legs, and abdomen. Heat exhaustion is more serious. Symptoms include headache, dizziness, severe fatigue, nausea, low urinary output, and weak and rapid

pulse. If you experience any of these symptoms, you should cool off and drink fluids containing potassium. Heat stroke causes hot, dry, flushed skin, incoherent behavior, inability to perspire, and seizures. If not treated, heat stroke can be fatal so medical attention is required immediately. To reduce the risk of heat injuries, drink 8 to 10 eight-ounce glasses of water per day and avoid extreme activity in the heat of the day or in an overly hot dance studio.

The Main Pointe

Training too frequently, too intensely, or for long durations may predispose you to injuries. Never "work through the pain." Learn your body's patterns and imbalances and seek help to correct them. Spend extra time on strength and flexibility. Seek the appropriate treatment from a qualified sports medicine professional or physical therapist.

7. Mental Preparation for Dance

—with Charee Boulter, PhD, Psychologist

Stage Fright

Most dancers fear they will experience stage fright. You might have an image of yourself — backstage before a performance with butterflies in your stomach, fearing you will fall during the performance. Your image might include the audience laughing or your fellow dancers being angry with you. Whatever your mental picture is of a failed performance, your ability to imagine it helps you understand why dancers sometimes experience stage fright.

It is important to know that even the best dancers experience anxiety or stage fright. How a dancer manages her anxiety is one of the keys to success. At the elite level, all of the performers are highly skilled and talented. They have spent years dancing and many hours rehearsing their performances. When you watch them onstage, the dancers with poise, grace and confidence who appear to be one with the music are the performers who are mentally prepared.

> *I get more anxious before my solos than I do for group dances. Every time I dance this gets a little better so I think I am working through it. There used to be a boy at my studio that would throw up every time he did his solo. The teacher would wait off-stage with a plastic*

bag. If you are this nervous it might help to talk to a counselor. —Emily, Age 16

All of us get in a circle before we dance and say something to encourage everyone. This helps us focus and bond as a team before we go onstage. Sometimes we get emotional and this adds intensity and depth to our performance. —Katie, Age 17

Benefits of Mental Preparation

Stage fright, stress, or anxiety is a part of life. Learning to manage anxiety as a dancer will help you improve your artistic abilities and will help you manage stress in other aspects of your life. Great success occurs when a dancer believes in the possibility in addition to her dedication, rehearsal and talent.

Here is a list of some of the positive benefits of mental preparation:
• Increased self confidence

• Improved focus during rehearsals and onstage

• Decreased fear and anxiety

• Increased enjoyment of dancing

• Enhanced performance

• Improved ability to manage stress

Aspects of Mental Preparation

Create a positive frame of mind:
Our way of thinking, positively or negatively, impacts the outcome of our efforts. When you maintain a positive focus you increase the likelihood of success. Consider the effect of steering while riding a bicycle. You steer in the direction that you want to go. Likewise, positive thinking is "steering" your mind and body in the direction you want to take your dancing.

The first step in creating a positive approach is to be aware of your thoughts.

• Notice when you have positive and negative thoughts

• Notice how you feel when you have positive thoughts

• Notice how you feel when you have negative thoughts

Many dancers feel energized and relaxed when they have positive thoughts. Negative thoughts often lead to feeling nervous, stressed, tired, or unmotivated.

Be aware that both negative and positive thoughts are normal parts of life. The goal of creating a positive mindset is not to remove all negative thoughts or judgments. Some of our negative thoughts are important judgments that help us. For example, when preparing a snack you notice the food you are about to eat has a strange smell and your thought is "This food is rotten!" This negative judgment is important and will help you avoid becoming ill. However, negative thoughts can hurt your performance. If you are struggling and find yourself thinking, "I will never get this. I am so uncoordinated," then your mindset is interfering with your ability to learn the choreography.

Recognize that your thoughts are just thoughts—not predictions of reality.
Reframe your negative thoughts that interfere with your performance into positive thoughts or challenges.

An example:
"I just can't get this new move."

When you recognize this is just a thought you can reframe it and create a positive challenge. "I am aware that I am struggling with this new move. I wonder what I can do differently to learn it. Maybe this is an opportunity to work with my dance instructor to enhance my flexibility."

By changing how you think about a situation you direct your attention toward your goal. You want to steer your mind's eye (thoughts) in the direction that you ultimately want to go.

Set Goals

Think about what you would ideally like to be doing as a dancer in five years. Go ahead and Dream Big! Remember, believing in the possibility is a key ingredient to your success. Write your goal down. Keep this someplace where you can see it. Sometimes we get so busy with daily life that we lose sight of our dreams and settle for less. Even if you don't achieve your dream goal, you will achieve at higher levels by setting your sights high. If your goal is only one or two steps above your current level you will limit your possibilities.

Look at your five-to-ten-year goal. What do you think is involved in achieving it? Talk to your dance instructor to find out what you need to do. Talk to your parents to see if they can support you in achieving this goal. Make a list of what you need to do and set smaller, intermediate goals.

An example:
"I want to audition and make the small groups in my Senior Dance Company."

Dance instructor's feedback:
—*Need to dance 3 to 4 hours daily*
—*Need to take two additional classes weekly*
—*Need to attend intensive dance camps during the summer*

Parents' feedback:
—*Supportive of increased daily practice, if I can still maintain my academic progress and household responsibilities*
—*Financially, they can support summer dance camp or increased weekly lessons*
—*They offer their support and suggest maintaining both my dance and academic goals*

Now focus on today and the next six months. It is important to have goals to guide you today. You should have a few goals specific to dancing. It is also important to include aspects of your life that are related, such as getting enough sleep, eating right, and finding a way to balance time with school, family, friends and dance.

Examples of Shorter-term Goals:

• Increase dance practice by two hours a day, beginning in two months after the next set of exams in school

- Talk to school counselor for ideas about time management so I can maintain my grades while dancing more

- Stop by school office next week and schedule the appointment for next two weeks

- Develop a financial plan with my parents and come up with ways to raise money to attend summer intensives and dance camps

- Share my goals and plans with friends to increase dance time

- Schedule quality time with friends so we keep the friendships active, while seeing less of each other

Positive Affirmations

Positive affirmations help you maintain your focus in the moment. They are short statements you repeat to yourself. Affirmations can help you manage anxiety and steer your mind in the direction you want to go.

Affirmations are stated positively, rather than focusing on what you want to avoid. Affirmations are about who you are becoming as a dancer. They help you build confidence in your possibilities and in your current abilities.

Examples of Affirmations:

—I am graceful.

—My legs are strong, my leaps are high.

—My legs are turned out.

—My feet are pointed and beautiful.

—My jumps are powerful.

—My kicks and extensions are amazing.

—My hips are down on my attitude.

—My relevé is high when I turn.

—My face is expressive and pleasing to the audience.

—I am good at feeling the music when I dance.

—My dance routine flows naturally from one move to the next.

—I dance with confidence and without hesitations or caution.

—I am great at learning new choreography.

—I enjoy having friends with the same passion for dance.

—Our dance company is synchronized and dancing as one.

Focus on goals while rehearsing

Prior to rehearsals, review your short-term goals and your affirmations. Make an effort to dance in the studio as if you were onstage. Dance with the grace and poise of a professional dancer. It is important to be mentally focused and physically disciplined. The more often you rehearse as if you are onstage, the easier it is to make the transition to the stage. You want to practice with intentions of greatness to train your body to perform onstage with grace.

Concentration

Some days it can be difficult to focus on dance. You may have an important test to study for or maybe you had a disagreement with a friend. When you find that your mind is wandering during rehearsal, try to refocus. This may be challenging. Here are some strategies that can help:

• Remind yourself that now is the time for dance (you can study when you leave the studio)

• Make time to deal with the stressor (time to study, time to talk to your friend)

• Focus on your dance instructor's voice when your mind wanders

• Focus on your breathing when your mind wanders

One of the best pieces of advice I have ever gotten is about learning to accept rejection and not let it affect my self esteem. If you can learn to work hard and motivate yourself while you are not getting the roles, awards, etc. it will serve you in the long run. It will set you apart from other dancers.

—Tracie Stanfield, Teacher at Broadway Dance Center,, Choreographer, Director of Synthesis Dance Project in NYC

The goal is to bring your attention back to your dancing. If you are dancing and thinking about other aspects of your life, you are not fully focused. In this state you are more likely to get injured and less likely to learn the dance as well as you can.

It is important that you deal with the issue creating the distraction. If you use dance as a place to escape, the issue will not resolve itself.

Visual Imagery

Using your imagination to create a perfect performance allows you the opportunity to rehearse mentally. Recall the beginning of the chapter when you imagined falling during a performance. If you can imagine a mistake and feel the related embarrassment and anxiety then you can imagine a perfect performance. Using visual imagery is similar to using positive thinking. It is important to visualize your desired performance.

Visual imagery is an important component of mental preparation. When you imagine your performance your muscles are activated, thus by imagining your desired performance, you are priming your muscles to repeat the performance.

Many dancers find it is easier to learn how to practice visualization after experiencing guided visualization. Ask your dance instructor if she/he knows somebody who can teach you.

You can begin on your own by following these steps to achieve a relaxed state:

• Find a quiet place without distractions

• Do some deep breathing to help your body relax

• Focus your mind on the sensations of your body as you breathe in and out

• Notice any muscle tension and try to relax as you exhale

After relaxing for a few minutes begin visualizing your peak or desired performance. You may view yourself dancing, as if you were watching a video of yourself. Imagine the movements flowing easily, as if you were one with the music. You may notice at times as you visualize that you feel the dance and experience it from within rather than as a video. Either form of visualizing is effective.

Some dancers find that it takes awhile to visualize a complete performance. Begin with as much as you can visualize. You might work on visualizing a challenging part of the choreography. You might visualize feeling confident, and managing your anxiety on opening night. Use your imagination to help build your confidence in yourself and your dancing abilities.

Anxiety Management

Remember that anxiety is not necessarily good or bad. It is what you do with the experience of anxiety and the intensity of the anxiety that determines how it will affect you. The optimal level of anxiety is often described as excitement or anticipation. At this level, anxiety is motivating and exciting. Too much anxiety is experienced as stress, intimidation, or fear.

You can change your response to heightened anxiety through physical, mental or emotional channels. Try different strategies to determine what works best for you.

Physical

• Take several deep breaths to gain control of your breathing

• Imagine you are inhaling confidence and exhaling your fears

• Get outside and go for a walk

• Do some gentle stretches and notice how your body feels

• Take a break and have a snack

Mental

- Notice your anxious thoughts

- Remind yourself that thoughts are only thoughts, not inevitable realities

- Reframe your thoughts into challenges

- Break the situation down into manageable components you can solve

> Your personality is a large part of who you are as a dancer. Don't hold back... It is the division between people who dance, and those who perform.
>
> —Anthony LoCascio, Teacher, Choreographer, Performer, President: www.dance4teachers.com

Emotional

- Talk to a friend for support

- Think of someplace happy and safe that stirs up positive feelings

- Watch a funny movie—laughter changes your emotional and physical states

- Do something you know you are good at—creating a positive experience of competence helps counter anxiety

- Do something to help another person—this takes your mind off of your worries and you feel good about helping another

If you find that these strategies do not help you manage your anxiety, talk to your parents or dance instructor. It may be helpful to seek professional consultation by speaking to a counselor and/or a medical provider to determine if your experience is stage fright or a more significant anxiety disorder.

The Main Pointe

Overall, remember that mental preparation can help enhance your experience as a dancer. Being mentally prepared is not magical and does not take the place of physical rehearsals, injury prevention/rehabilitation, sound nutrition, or adequate sleep. It is a component of the complete dancer— attending to mind, body and emotion.

8. Help! I'm Stressed!

$\int$ tress. We all have it. Even dancers. Schoolwork, family issues, boyfriends, girlfriends, not enough sleep, pressure to make good grades, you name it. It can be positive or negative. However, too much of any stress can seriously affect our physical and mental well-being. Dancers may have trouble performing at an optimal level until they have dealt with their chronic stress. We now know much more about the "mind-body connection." It has been estimated that 60 to 70% of all diseases are in some way stress related. Eighty-nine percent of adults report that they experience high stress levels and 75 to 90% of doctor visits are stress related. To achieve total wellness and to be a great dancer, we must address all aspects of our lives and strive for balance.

What Does Stress Do To Your Body?

- The "Fight or Flight" Syndrome

- Immediate effects

- Increased breathing rate

- Increased heartrate and blood pressure

- Fats and sugars are released into your blood stream

- Increased blood clotting

- Increased cortisol (a hormone related to stress)

Long-Term Effects:

- Increased cholesterol

- Increased blood pressure

- Increased homocysteine (a measure of inflammation)

- Leads to constricted arteries and abnormal heart rhythms

- Compromised immune system

- Poor memory

- Increased drug abuse and alcoholism

- Increased obesity and overweight

- Stomach and digestive problems

- Grinding teeth, nervous habits

Stress Vulnerability

Recent research has focused on "stress vulnerability." Two people may have the same stressors and problems but one gets sick and one stays well. Why is this? Changing our physical and mental response to the stress is what is important. Research shows that people who adhere to the following behaviors stay well and develop fewer stress-related diseases. The same things you do to become a better dancer also protect you from the effects of stress in your life.

• Eat a balanced and nutritious diet

• Exercise regularly

• Get plenty of rest and sleep

• Avoid abuse of alcohol, tobacco, or drugs

• Organize your life and have a plan for your finances

• Surround yourself with positive people and friends you can count on in times of stress

• Take control of situations and make firm commitments to projects you care about

• Nurture your spiritual life

• Laugh often—see the humor in every situation

• Learn to get rid of anger, hostility, and resentment. Get professional help if necessary

• Focus on concerns that have a solution instead of worrying about things you cannot change

• Be assertive and make your needs known to others in an honest and polite manner

• Exercise your brain: read, do puzzles, play games, and visit museums

• Travel and see the world, go on vacation

• Be adventurous—keep the creative spark

• Get a pet—walk a dog whether you own one or not

• Design your castle — your room should reflect the true you and give you serenity

• Volunteer — it takes the focus off of you and it helps others

Dance, Exercise, and Stress Management

Exercise is one of the best ways to control and reduce the stress in your life. Activity provides a diversion; getting you away from the source of stress to clear your mind and to sort through the problems. Regular exercise makes you look and feel better about yourself. Others will notice your improved self-concept. Physiological changes that occur with long-term, regular activity provide more strength, endurance, and energy to cope with difficult situations. Muscular tension, which builds up throughout a stressful day, is easily released with aerobic activity and stretching.

These physiological changes are also consistent with disease prevention. Exercise can reverse and/or improve many of the health problems that are related to stress. Benefits can include decreased blood pressure, lowered cholesterol, reduced stress hormones, and improved sleeping patterns. Other benefits can include improvement in depression and mood and the lowering of body fat and weight. If you ever stop dancing, quickly replace your activity with exercise that you enjoy.

Stress Reduction and Relaxation

Mindful Breathing—A simple deep breath or two can promote an immediate relaxation response. Deep breathing should not happen in your chest but in the abdominal area. Your diaphragm will lower and your abdominals will push out. Take time out for sixty seconds when things get tense. Close your eyes and focus on your breathing. When your "To Do List" sneaks into your mind, just go back and focus on your breathing.

Meditation—Follow the instructions for mindful breathing but choose an object or word to focus on. Empty your mind of everything else. And just slowly repeat the word mentally, over and over again.

Mental Imagery—During or after the final stretch of your workout or dance class, clear your mind and focus on one single image. This could be a shape, a color, your favorite place or anything you associate with quiet and peace. It is simply a "mental vacation." It takes practice to avoid letting your mind wander to other things. Combine this technique with slow, deep breathing.

Visualization—By using mental pictures you can change attitudes and behaviors. Improve your organization by imagining what your room will look like when it is in order or improve your posture by imagining puppet strings attached to the top of your head and shoulders.

Progressive Muscle Relaxation—Progressive relaxation trains your muscles to release tension as it builds up instead of storing it throughout the day. Lie in a comfortable position (on your back or on your side with bent knees). Close your eyes. Start by taking several deep, slow breaths. Now, as you breath in, you are going to tense a muscle or muscle group, as you exhale let the muscle relax. Focus on how different it feels in the tense state versus the relaxed state.

Follow this sequence:
• Inhale—flex your right foot

• Exhale—let it relax

• Inhale—flex your left foot

• Exhale—let it go

Repeat with the following contractions, inhaling and exhaling slowly each time:

• Flex your feet and tense calf muscles

• Tighten both legs and press them together

• Tighten the thighs

• Tighten the buttocks

• Pull in the abdominal area and flatten the back

• Tense your chest and shrug your shoulders.

• Clench your fists and press your arms into the floor.

• Close your eyes tight and contract your jaw and facial muscles.

If you still feel tension in an area, continue contacting and relaxing until the tightness disappears.

Massage—Treat yourself to massage therapy or take turns rubbing your friends' shoulders in dance class. Research demonstrates many valuable health and stress-reducing benefits from massage.

The Main Pointe

Be good to yourself. This is it. You only get one body and one life. Treat them right. Balance your dance life, school life, friend life and family life. Other stress-reducing tactics include seeking help when you feel overwhelmed, practicing time management, and finding someone you trust to talk to. Seek opportunities that offer personal growth and discovery. Remember that you are special. Focus on relaxation, enjoyment, and health.

9. Fruits and Veggies for Oxidative Stress

Affter a long dance class, rehearsal, or performance you feel tired but good. Although you are working hard and getting stronger and more flexible there is also something going on inside your cells. Your cells are being attacked by the very oxygen you breathe. Chemical reactions in your body produce oxidants that are called free radicals. These free radicals are missing an electron which makes them very unstable. They run around your body trying to "steal" an electron from your healthy molecules. This can cause damage to cell membranes, red blood cells, muscle fibers, proteins and even your DNA (your blueprint to make more cells). The free radicals cause a chain reaction of destruction to your cells. By attacking cell membranes, they cause cellular damage, muscle fatigue, injury and vulnerability to chronic disease. Everyone has oxidative stress but athletes and dancers have excessive amounts. As intensity and duration increase—oxidative damage increases. So while exercise and dance are good for you, you need to prevent long-term damage. By eating the right foods (antioxidants) you can stabilize and stop the free radical damage.

Some diseases linked by research to oxidative stress:
—*Cardiovascular disease*
—*Cancer*

—*Lung disease*
—*Macular Degeneration (eyes)*
—*Diabetes*
—*Arthritis*
—*Alzheimer's disease*
—*Parkinson's disease*
—*Cataracts*
—*Poor immune system*
—*Wrinkling and skin damage*

**Other things that produce free radicals
and oxidative stress:**
—*Alcohol consumption*
—*UV light from the sun*
—*Smoking or second-hand smoke*
—*Psychological stress*
—*Toxins in the environment*
—*Illness and injury*

How to Eat the Right Foods to get Antioxidants

There are thousands of nutrients in fruits, vegetables, beans, and grains. These are called "phytochemicals" or "phytonutrients". We will call them "PHYTOS" for short. There are different "PHYTOS" for each color of fruits and vegetables. So broccoli has different "PHYTOS" than sweet potatoes or blueberries. These "PHYTOS" have all the antioxidants you need to neutralize the free radicals and to stop damage to your body. Research and our government guidelines recommend 9 to 13 RAW fruits and vegetables in a rainbow of colors to be in your diet every day. This is what it takes to prevent disease, prevent damage to your proteins, and to build your immune system. Isolated, man-made vitamins have not been found to be effective except in higher, toxic doses (e.g. side effects like kidney damage). You have to get antioxidants from your food. Each color of fruits and vegetables has different nutrients.  They all have important roles in human nutrition and in maintaining health. One apple has over ten thousand identified "PHYTOS." These nutrients work in a delicate balance to perform all of the  important functions in the cells of your body. You cannot get this from a man-made vitamin pill. If you know you don't eat the recommended amount every day, try a whole food supplement that is actually made from real juiced fruits and vegetables. See the next chapter and the Recommended Resources for information on Juice Plus+® which is the one I recommend to my clients. Choose fruits and vegetables with a lot of color: dark green, purple and blue, deep orange and red. Don't forget the nuts, seeds, and whole grains.

Dancers Should Eat the Rainbow Every Day!!!

According to the new food guide pyramid, teenage athletes need 9 to 13 different colors of raw fruits and veggies every single day:

Blue and Purple—great at stopping those free radicals.

—*Blackberries*
—*Blueberries*
—*Black currants*
—*Dried plums*
—*Elderberries*
—*Purple figs*
—*Purple grapes*
—*Plums*
—*Raisins*

—*Purple asparagus*
—*Purple cabbage*
—*Purple carrots*
—*Eggplant*
—*Purple Belgian endive*
—*Purple peppers*
—*Potatoes (purple fleshed)*
—*Black salsify*

Go for the Green!—Lowers risk of cancer, protects your
vision, and builds strong bones and teeth.

—*Avocados*	—*Green cabbage*
—*Green apples*	—*Celery*
—*Green grapes*	—*Chayote squash*
—*Honeydew melon*	—*Cucumbers*
—*Kiwi*	—*Endive*
—*Limes*	—*Leafy greens*
—*Green pears*	—*Leeks*
	—*Lettuce*
—*Artichokes*	—*Green onion*
—*Arugula*	—*Okra*
—*Asparagus*	—*Peas*
—*Broccoflower*	—*Green pepper*
—*Broccoli*	—*Snow peas*
—*Broccoli rabe*	—*Sugar snap peas*
—*Brussels sprouts*	—*Spinach*
—*Chinese cabbage*	—*Watercress*
—*Green beans*	—*Zucchini*

WHITE is Right!—Good for your heart and lowers cancer risk

—*Bananas*
—*Brown pears*
—*Dates*
—*White nectarines*
—*White peaches*

—*Cauliflower*
—*Garlic*
—*Ginger*
—*Jerusalem artichoke*

—*Jicama*
—*Kohlrabi*
—*Mushrooms*
—*Onions*
—*Parsnips*
—*Potatoes (white fleshed)*
—*Shallots*
—*Turnips*
—*White Corn*

YELLOW and ORANGE—Builds your immune system and improves health in every way

—*Yellow apples*
—*Apricots*
—*Cantaloupe*
—*Cape gooseberries*
—*Yellow figs*
—*Grapefruit*
—*Golden kiwi*
—*Lemon*

—*Mangoes*
—*Nectarines*
—*Oranges*
—*Papayas*
—*Peaches*
—*Yellow pears*
—*Persimmons*
—*Pineapples*

—*Tangerines*
—*Yellow watermelon*

—*Yellow beets*
—*Butternut squash*
—*Carrots*
—*Yellow peppers*
—*Yellow potatoes*
—*Pumpkin*

—*Rutabagas*
—*Yellow summer squash*
—*Sweet corn*
—*Sweet potatoes*
—*Yellow tomatoes*
—*Yellow winter squash*

I SAID RED—Helps you remember things, prevents urinary tract problems, and protects your heart

—*Red apples*
—*Blood oranges*
—*Cherries*
—*Cranberries*
—*Red grapes*
—*Pink/red grapefruit*
—*Red pears*
—*Pomegranates*
—*Raspberries*
—*Strawberries*
—*Watermelon*

—*Beets*
—*Red peppers*
—*Radishes*
—*Radicchio*
—*Red onions*
—*Red potatoes*
—*Rhubarb*
—*Tomatoes*

10 Ways Dancers Can Eat More Fruits and Veggies:

1. Pack dried fruit like raisins, apricots, and figs in small
    bags with raw almonds in your dance bag.

2. Make a fruit or chocolate banana smoothie for breakfast
    or after dance.

3. Cut up veggies and make dip on the weekend so you can
    grab-and-go all week.

4. Keep a big bowl of apples, pears, and oranges on the
    counter to throw in your lunch for school or your dance
    bag. No packaging required.

5. Always eat fruit on your cereal (whole grain is best).

6. Order sides of veggies in restaurants. Almost all
    restaurants will bring you a side of broccoli or green
    beans.

7. See how colorful you can make your salad. Try for at
    least five different colors of veggies. Croutons and Bacon
    Bits don't count.

8. Learn to eat food with beans. Rice and beans and
    Mexican dishes are delicious.

9. Try 100% fruit juice instead of soda or other sugary drinks. Orange juice with calcium and vitamin D is a great choice.

10. Fresh pineapple has an enzyme that repairs muscle—it's a great snack after a hard class or rehearsal.

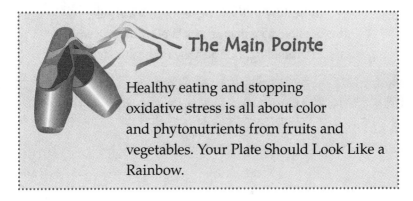

The Main Pointe

Healthy eating and stopping oxidative stress is all about color and phytonutrients from fruits and vegetables. Your Plate Should Look Like a Rainbow.

Athletes are often undernourished, although many of them eat lots of food. They often engage in eating patterns that may provide short-term benefits, but are unhealthy in the long-term. Fortunately, it is possible to enhance sports performance while building, not destroying health.

—Pamela A. Popper, PhD. ND

From *The Wellness Forum's Guide to Sports Nutrition*

10. Whole Food Nutrition for Dancers

The right diet can enhance your performance as a dancer and as a student and can help you lead a long and happy life. The real news is not that a healthy diet is good for you—we all know that—the real news is that a healthy diet may save your life. From the last chapter we now know that consuming a variety of the right foods lowers a person's risk for many chronic diseases and enhances the benefits gained through regular exercise and dance training. Dance workouts combined with proper nutrition will aid in weight control, help reduce calcium loss from bones, and reduce the negative effects of stress and anxiety. No matter what your personal goals for dance are, a nutrition plan is essential.

It can be difficult to make these changes when most of your friends are feasting on fast food and pizza. It takes discipline and planning to eat an optimal diet day in and day out. The good news is that the same dietary changes that make you a better dancer will also build your immune system and protect you from illness and disease. A few carefully made changes can modify your nutritional habits for a lifetime of optimal health and maximal performance.

What Should I Eat?

All individuals should consume a plant-based diet with about 65 to 70% of calories from carbohydrates, 15% of calories from protein and 15 to 20% from fat. Dancers simply need more calories than the average person because of their activity level. The proportion of each nutrient in the diet remains the same. So the entire family can make these changes together. The research is very clear that the same dietary choices that prevent cancer and heart disease also reduce your risk of obesity, eye disease, Alzheimer's, Parkinson's, and many other lifestyle-related diseases. The changes are not all easy but they are simple. If your favorite food is high in fat and sugar you will need to save it for very special occasions or possibly decrease the quantity. If you really savor the taste, you may not need such a large portion. Go for quality—not quantity.

The information in this book is intended as a general guideline for the dancer and the rest of the family. If you have any medical conditions or are taking any medications, it is important to consult a registered dietitian and your physician for specific advice.

Carbohydrates

Carbohydrates are the most important nutrient for exercising muscles and are needed for optimal brain and central nervous system function. The recommended amount of carbohydrate for athletes and dancers is 65 to 70% of your total caloric intake. Carbohydrates are necessary nutrients but it is important to consume the right kind. Refined sugars and starches like white bread, sodas, cookies, donuts, and candy have little nutritional value and are quickly absorbed and stored as fat. Because these sugary foods are digested so quickly, they overload the blood with glucose.

Complex carbohydrates are foods that are left in their whole state—whole grains, fruits, vegetables, and legumes (beans). They still have the vitamins, minerals and fiber intact and they take much longer to be broken down. The sugars are released much more slowly into the bloodstream avoiding excess glucose in the blood. The average person consumes 158 pounds of sugar every year with much of it coming in the beverages we drink. A 20-ounce Coca-Cola® has 16.25 teaspoons of sugar, and a Pepsi® has 28 teaspoons. A 10-ounce Dannon® Frusion Yogurt has 11.75 teaspoons of sugar and a McDonald's® vanilla shake has 12 teaspoons in a 20-ounce portion.

How Sugar Harms: Ten Good Reasons for an Athlete to Avoid Simple Sugars

1. Sugar can suppress the immune system.

2. Sugar can cause difficulty with concentration and promote hyperactivity and anxiety.

3. Sugar can upset the mineral balance in the body.

4. Sugar can produce a rise in your triglycerides and a decrease in your good cholesterol, leading to decreased health.

5. Sugar can feed cancer growth.

6. Sugar contributes to the reduction in defense against bacterial infections.

7. Too much sugar can lead to a chromium deficiency.

8. Sugar can increase fasting levels of glucose.

9. Sugar can cause hypoglycemia.

10. Sugar can produce an acidic digestive tract.

Fiber
Eating a lot of complex carbohydrates will automatically give you enough fiber. Fiber refers to the components of plant cell walls that are not digested by human intestinal enzymes. It is also called "roughage" or "bulk." When whole grains are processed or refined, much of the fiber is removed and many of the nutrients are lost. Fiber adds bulk to the diet, absorbs water in the intestine and produces larger, softer stools that are easily eliminated. This decreases the time that cancer-causing agents are in contact with the lining of the

large intestine and colon. This also inhibits the absorption of toxins into the bloodstream. People who consume a high-fiber diet have less colon cancer, heart disease, cholesterol problems, and gallstones. Soluble fiber forms a gel as it moves through the digestive system, interfering with the absorption of cholesterol. Oat bran, oatmeal, barley, rice bran, apples, oranges, strawberries, prunes, carrots, corn, broccoli, lentils, navy beans, and pinto beans all contain soluble fiber. Fiber of any kind is also great for weight loss as it fills the stomach and decreases appetite.

Dancers are the world's supreme athletes. You must eat as if you are an athlete training for the Olympics. Good nutrition and great dancing go hand in hand. You can't have one without the other. Maintain optimum health and condition year round. If you have questions about how to eat, consult a nutritionist.

—Jeff Amsden, Dancer, Choreographer, TV, Stage and Film Performer, Faculty at Broadway Dancer Center

Conditions sometimes associated with low-fiber diets are chronic constipation, diverticulitis, irritable bowel syndrome, Crohn's Disease, colitis, and blood clots in veins and lungs. Cancer, heart disease, diabetes, and kidney problems have all been linked to low-fiber diets.

The optimal diet should have about 45 g of fiber a day. Fruits, vegetables, legumes (beans), nuts, whole-grain breads, cereals and rice are great choices.

Protein

The job of protein is to build and repair body tissues, including muscles, tendons, and ligaments. It is also necessary for the synthesis of hormones, enzymes, and antibodies, as well as for fluid transport and energy. It is very rare in developed nations, especially the United States, for there to be a deficiency in protein intake. Most of us eat too much protein, especially animal protein, and choose poor quality sources. Research suggests that an active adult needs about 15% of their calories to be comprised of protein. Excess protein puts stress on the digestive tract, kidneys, and liver. Too much protein from animal sources causes an excess of uric acid in the bloodstream. Uric acid is a by-product of protein metabolism. In order to neutralize this acid, the body steals calcium from bones and other stores within the body, leeching the body of calcium. Some nutritionists believe the reason we need such a high intake of calcium is because of our excessive intake of protein, especially protein from animal sources. Some even implicate the rise in osteoporosis with the increase of protein in our diets. The Nutrition Committee of the Council on Nutrition, Physical Activity, and Metabolism of the American Heart Association states, "High-protein diets are not recommended because they restrict healthful foods that provide essential nutrients and do not provide the variety of foods needed to adequately meet nutritional needs. Individuals who follow these diets are therefore at risk for compromised vitamin and mineral intake, as well as potential cardiac, renal, bone, and liver abnormalities overall."

Your caloric intake is directly linked to performance, recovery, normal growth and development, and body weight goals. The young athlete has nutritional requirements that are greater than average people. These requirements can be met by eating 5 to 7 small, nutrient-dense meals throughout the day. Make sure you follow a sports-specific nutrition program, consume enough calories, and get adequate periods of rest and recovery. Remember, NO PAIN, NO GAIN and TRAIN UNTIL YOU DROP is for fools.

—From *PowerPack for the Winning Edge*, by Jack A. Medina, MA and Roy E. Vartabedian, PhD

Can athletes and dancers be vegetarians? Will they grow and perform just as well on plant foods? Yes. You can easily get the protein you need from fruits, vegetables, soy foods, beans, grains, seeds, and nuts. Fish, like wild salmon, is an excellent source as well. Consume only protein supplements and energy bars made from plant protein such as soy-based smoothie mixes (see Recommended Resources). Research indicates that if you can keep your intake of animal foods to less than 10% of your caloric intake, your risk of disease goes down dramatically. This means you don't have to be a complete vegetarian but it's best to move in that direction to protect your health. Think of animal food as a small condiment-sized serving instead of the main part of your plate. This means you can get excellent protein from plant sources for many of your meals. Nuts, seeds, grains, beans, and soy products all contain high-quality protein. If you choose to eat beef and poultry choose organic, low-fat varieties and do not consume the skin. Free-range and grass-fed sources are best. Free-range eggs are a better choice as they have a higher ratio of omega-3 fatty acids. If you can purchase organic animal foods it will reduce your consumption of steroids, antibiotics, growth hormone residues, etc.

> Dancers work and live from the inside. They drive themselves constantly—producing a glow that lights not only themselves but also audience after audience.
>
> —M. Louis

Protein is not what builds muscle. Training is what builds muscle. Eating a balanced, plant-based diet will give your body the building blocks it needs to do its thing. With the right choices, dancers can perform at a high level and still protect themselves from developing diseases in the future.

Fat

Fat is the primary fuel you use for light-to-moderate-intensity exercise. You should not consume more than 15 to 20% of your total calories from fat. The essential fatty acids provided by the fat in your diet are important for maintaining healthy cell membranes, healthy skin, making hormones, and transporting certain vitamins. The proper type of fat is the important thing.

Reduce Saturated Fat and Cholesterol

Animal food is the primary source for saturated fat in the diet. Fat on beef, pork, veal, the skin on poultry, dairy products like cheese, milk, lard, and butter, are all common sources of saturated fats. It is also found in palm oil, palm kernel oil, and coconut oil. There is overwhelming research showing that diets high in saturated fats raise the risk of heart disease, stroke, and many forms of cancer. One of the hardest foods to reduce is cheese. Cheese is very high in saturated fat and is included in almost everything we eat in the typical American diet.

Avoid Trans-Fat or Hydrogenated Fat

These are fats, which have been altered to make food products have a longer shelf life. They are very damaging and are mostly found in cookies, cakes, crackers, fast food, and other highly processed foods. Trans fatty acids are very hard for your body to break down. They stick together causing fatty deposits in the arteries and the liver. Like saturated fat, they are associated with a higher incidence of heart disease and stroke and depress the immune system. If the label says a food has trans fat—Put it back! There are plenty of other choices without it.

The Good Fats
The best choices are monounsaturated fats like olive oil and canola oil. Good fats come from nuts, seeds, flax, avocados, and olives. Remember that all oils are equally high in calories. Carry a bag of raw almonds and walnuts in your dance bag.

Omega-3 Fatty Acids
Every cell in our body needs omega-3 fatty acids to function optimally. We cannot manufacture them ourselves so they must be ingested. The omega-6 fatty acids are also essential but our modern diets contain plenty of this oil. During the last century people in developed countries like the United States have eliminated almost all omega-3 fatty acids from their diet. Where we used to have a ratio of one omega-6 to one omega-3, we now have a ratio of 20 omega-6s to one omega-3.

What do omega-3 fatty acids do in the body? They help control energy production in the cell and they are the building blocks of your cell membranes, controlling what comes in and out of the cell.

Research has discovered that this depletion of omega-3
has had a very negative effect on our bodies, particularly
on the brain and the heart. The rise in heart disease and
depression has directly paralleled this decrease in omega-
3 consumption. Other diseases related to this deficiency
are rheumatoid arthritis, diabetes, postpartum depression,
cancer, obesity, asthma, attention disorders, and aggression/
hostility in teenagers.

> Why do I dance? Why do you breathe?
>
> —From a Dance T-shirt

There used to be an abundance of omega-3 fatty acids in the
food supply especially in populations that ate fish and wild
game. When cows and chickens were allowed to roam free
and eat grass, the meat and eggs had a much higher content of
omega-3's. Because our food supply has changed drastically,
people now consume little or no omega-3's. Salmon that is
farm-raised has no chance to eat the algae, which makes wild,
fatty fish high in this essential nutrient. Fish have also been
contaminated with environmental pollutants like mercury
and PCBs, which make it less desirable to eat the amounts
needed to get adequate omega-3's.

How to Get More Omega-3

- Increase omega-3 fatty acids in your diet and decrease
  omega-6-containing oils (corn oil, safflower oil and
  sunflower oil).

• Good sources of omega-3's are:

• Flax and hemp seeds (grind whole seeds in your coffee grinder)

• Walnuts

• Soy foods/tofu

• Oily fish (salmon, mackerel, tuna)

• Fortified eggs or eggs from free-range/ grass fed chickens

• Wild game

• Flaxseed oil

• High quality/Purified fish oil Supplements (Risky because they can oxidize or spoil and can have contaminants. See Recommended Resources for more information and check with your physician before consuming a supplement)

Do Dancers Need Supplements? Whole Food versus Man-Made?

Researchers are beginning to understand that vitamin supplements cannot make up for a poor diet and that supplements have not been shown to cure any disease. In several studies, isolated, man-made supplements were found to cause more harm than good. If you think about this it makes sense. Our bodies need thousands of nutrients, so eating the whole food item works better than pulling out one nutrient and hoping that it will work by itself. We need to eat food in the way it was put on earth—whole and unprocessed.

The government and other researchers have spent billions of dollars and dozens of years trying to find a cure for heart disease, cancer and other diseases. They have tried to discover what is the one thing in the orange that is good for you. After years of study we now know that it is the synergy of the whole orange that allows your body to function at its very best. Food should be eaten in the proportion in which it was put on earth, not in fragmented, isolated vitamins or man-made elements. There is overwhelming evidence that people who eat a variety of raw fruits, raw vegetables and unrefined grains have the least amount of disease. The problem is that very few humans actually consume the necessary amount and variety of these healthy foods.

Guidelines for Choosing a Supplement
(excerpted from *PowerPack for the Winning Edge* by Roy
E. Vartabedian, PhD and Jack A. Medina, M.A. See
Recommended Resources)

1. Are you sure the product does not contain any harmful
    or "extra" ingredients? Just because it is natural does
    not mean it is safe. Recently, popular children's vitamins
    were found to contain lead.

2. Does the supplement contain whole foods from real
    fruits, vegetables, and grains or is it made of isolated,
    man-made vitamins?

3. Does it contain ingredients that have no proven benefit?
    Testimonials are abundant but there is no real gold-
    standard, peer-reviewed, published research showing
    that the supplement is absorbed and has benefits in the
    body.

4. Is the research on the actual product and not a selected
    ingredient? Does the research show benefits in the
    human body (not rats)? Is there a placebo group (one
    group gets the real thing and the other gets a sugar pill)?
    Is it double-blind (nobody knows who got what until
    the study is over)? Is it published in a peer-reviewed
    scientific journal (real science)?

5. Does the company that makes the supplement make fantastic or unbelievable claims about their product? Words like "miracle", "cure", amazing", secret formula", and testimonials about diseases that were cured should raise red flags. Only prescription drugs may claim to treat or cure diseases, not supplements.

Whole Food Supplements

People know they should eat more fruits and vegetables but in reality it is not happening. If you know you do not eat 9 to 13 fruits and vegetables each day, the best insurance is a whole food supplement. This is especially important for dancers because of the extra oxidative stress from training so hard. I recommend one to my clients called Juice Plus+®. Taking Juice Plus+® capsules every day provides the nutritional foundation we so desperately need and that is so lacking in our diets today. Juice Plus+® is not a vitamin supplement, providing a limited number of handpicked nutrients. Juice Plus+® is a whole food based product providing the wide array of nutrients found in a variety of nutritious fruits, vegetables, and grains. It's the next best thing to fruits and vegetables...because we don't get nearly enough of the real thing every day. Juice Plus+® comes in capsules, chewables, and gummies. It is certified as gluten-free and is kosher. This is one of the very few supplements that I recommend because it has a large body of primary, peer-reviewed research to show that it improves immune function, improves circulation, lowers inflammation, and reduces oxidative stress in normal people and in athletes. Juice Plus+® has been analyzed to determine what's in it, where it goes in the body, and what it does when it gets there. This is very rare in the supplement world. Juice Plus+® is the perfect answer for those of us who try hard in our busy lives but don't always get the recommended 9 to 13 fruits and veggies into our systems every day. See the Recommended Resources section for ordering information.

Protecting the Dancer's Bones

Bones are living tissues, constantly being remodeled and reacting to hormonal changes, nutrition, and stressors applied to them. Osteoporosis is a disease in which low bone mass and deterioration of bone structure causes bones to be weak, porous, brittle, and susceptible to fracture. At highest risk are Asian and Caucasian females who are relatively thin and sedentary, postmenopausal women without estrogen support, and those with a family history of osteoporosis. Black females are at lower risk, probably because of greater bone mass. Men can develop osteoporosis but it usually shows up much later in life.

Researchers are beginning to realize that the main cause of osteoporosis is a high intake of acidic food, mainly animal protein. The higher the intake of protein, the more uric acid is produced, which must be neutralized by calcium from bones and teeth. Animal products and processed foods contain high levels of phosphorous which also has to be neutralized with calcium. Osteoporosis is linked with kidney disorders because of the high stress on the kidneys to eliminate the leftovers from protein metabolism. The answer is to eat a diet high in fruits and vegetables that have a high calcium-to-phosphorous ratio. Plant-based calcium is much more available, prevents leeching of calcium from bones and teeth, and is easily absorbed. Try to increase tofu, soy products (processed with calcium sulfate or calcium chloride), raw almonds, calcium-fortified orange juice, bok choy, broccoli, kale, turnip greens, parsley, mustard greens, and endive. Calcium must have vitamin D in order to function, so consume foods fortified with added Vitamin D like orange juice, soy milk, and cereals. Other foods with vitamin D include egg yolks, salmon, and sardines. Exposure to sunshine for 10 to 15 minutes without sunscreen allows your body to make its own vitamin D. Never stay out long enough to burn.

No one can arrive from being talented alone, work transforms talent into genius.

—Anna Pavlova

What About Dairy Foods?
The only drink that is biologically necessary after weaning is water. Recent research is finding that dairy products may not be the health food that we once thought it was. Dairy foods are a huge source of saturated fat. Whole milk is 49%

fat and 2% milk derives 35% of its calories from fat. Most cheeses are about 70% fat. Saturated fat is linked to insulin resistance, higher cholesterol, heart disease, and stroke. Dairy sugar is called lactose. About 55% of the calories in fat-free milk actually come from this sugar. Many people are lactose intolerant, which can cause severe stomach upset. Also, the protein in dairy foods has come under scrutiny for contributing to Type 1 diabetes, loss of kidney function in diabetics, prostate cancer, and ovarian cancer. Migraine sufferers and people with rheumatoid arthritis may find that dairy protein is a trigger for attacks.

Most people consume dairy for the calcium but it is very easy to get calcium from plant foods. You would be surprised how great soy milk, rice milk, and almond milk taste. Most of these come in vanilla, chocolate, and strawberry flavors. If you consume less animal protein in general, you will actually need less calcium anyway because your diet is more alkaline instead of acid.

Avoid These to Prevent Osteoporosis:
• Tobacco—Lowers hormone levels, thereby accelerating bone loss. Stopping smoking at any age slows bone loss.

• High caffeine intake—Increases the amount of calcium excreted in the urine, depriving the bones of calcium they need. Also, carbonated sodas have phosphates, which cause loss of calcium from bones and teeth.

- Alcohol—Suppresses bone tissue formation.

- Excessive dieting—Hurts the bones by depriving the body of important nutrients, including calcium. Eating disorders can also affect bone health.

- Excessive physical activity—Can cause bone loss by depressing hormone levels, evident when a female dancer begins to miss her normal menstrual periods (amenorrhea).

Strategies For Preventing Osteoporosis:

- Consume a calcium-rich diet—calcium is essential to healthy bones. This is extremely important during the teen years and early adulthood when we build our peak bone density, but also throughout our lives. Vegetable, nut and fish sources are best: almonds, calcium-fortified juice, tofu, soy products (processed with calcium or calcium chloride), bok choy, broccoli, kale, turnip greens, canned sardines, salmon with bones, and calcium supplements as needed.

- Vitamin D—necessary for our bodies to utilize calcium from sources such as: sunshine, fortified foods like orange juice, soy milk, rice milk, and cereals. Also found in: salmon, sardines, egg yolks, and Toni's Smoothie (Recipe can be found in Chapter 11).

- Weight Bearing Exercise—Dancing is perfect. Just add some strength training for the arms and upper body. Research shows this is very important for maintaining bone health.

- Consult a physician or registered dietitian—Learn about your risk for osteoporosis and the recommended treatment.

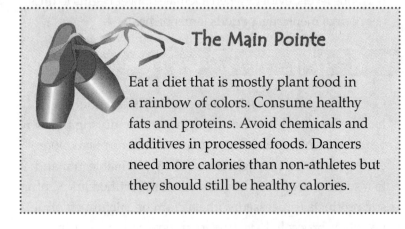

The Main Pointe

Eat a diet that is mostly plant food in a rainbow of colors. Consume healthy fats and proteins. Avoid chemicals and additives in processed foods. Dancers need more calories than non-athletes but they should still be healthy calories.

11. Eating In, Eating Out, and Shopping

What to Eat Before, During and After Dance

Carbohydrates like cereal, pasta, bread, rice, vegetables, and fruits are the main fuel for dance training and performance. Carbohydrates in the diet must replace glycogen in the liver and in muscles. Failure to recover glycogen stores leads to early fatigue, lower exercise intensity, and increased risk for illness and injury.

What to eat before dance class or a performance
The closer you eat to the time of performance or class, the smaller the meal should be. A heavy meal could lead to cramping and low energy. Your muscles are competing with your digestive system for blood flow and energy. Good pre-dance choices include fruit, pasta, baked potato, healthy snack bars, whole grain toast or English muffins with spreadable fruit. Poor choices include protein and high-fat foods that are slower to digest and can make you sluggish during your activity.

What to eat after dance class or a performance
Within 30 minutes of a hard training session (or as soon as possible) consume a meal or snack containing about 80% carbohydrate and 20% protein. A peanut butter and fruit spread sandwich, raw almonds and dried fruit, beans and

rice, pasta and veggies, or a fruit and protein smoothie (recipe on page 106) would be great.

What to eat during a competition or a long performance

Drink water between each number and take small bites to keep your energy up. Orange, kiwi, or apple slices, a banana, a couple of raisins, plain bread or a bagel would all work. Do not consume anything with a high fat or high protein content or a drink with a high sugar content.

Meal and Snack Ideas for Dancers in Training

• Whole-grain cereal (with fruit and soy, rice, or almond milk

• Sandwich on whole grain bread with hummus, spreadable fruit and peanut or almond butter, veggies, or organic turkey

• Brown or wild rice with veggies or beans

• Whole-grain tortilla wrap with veggies, beans and avocados

• Pita pocket with veggies, tuna, or hummus

• Pasta with veggies and/or tomato sauce

- Fruit of any kind (fresh pineapple has an enzyme that repairs muscle)

- Baked potato or sweet potato

- Oatmeal

- Raw almonds, pecans or walnuts mixed with dried fruit

- Parfait with fruit and granola

- Celery and peanut or almond butter

- Raw veggies with hummus or low-fat dip

- Baked tortilla chips with salsa

- Mini rice cakes with peanut or almond butter

- Graham crackers or ginger snaps dipped in applesauce

- Healthy sports bars/granola bars are preferable to fast food or vending machines (try Kashi® brand or a bar with low sugar, high-fiber, and a plant-based protein source)

- Homemade banana bread or muffins

- Juice Plus+ Complete® smoothie with fruit (recipe on page 106)

Healthy Recipes

Toni's Smoothie Recipe for Dancers (and Tired Parents)
This can be altered to fit your taste buds. It is a complete meal replacement, quick and healthy breakfast or after training snack, to reload muscle glycogen. This provides over half of your day's worth of calcium—all from plant sources. I have found that a good blender makes all the difference. My kids like it to be smooth. Play around with it until you find a recipe that you love.

French Vanilla Smoothie with Fruit

*1 cup of vanilla soymilk, rice milk, water, or calcium
    fortified juice*

*1 scoop of French Vanilla Juice Plus+ Complete® (see
    Recommended Resources to order)*

1 ripe banana

*1 Tablespoon brewer's yeast or nutritional yeast
    (provides B vitamins, important addition for
    vegetarians)*

*1 Tablespoon ground flaxseed for omega-3's (just put
    whole seeds in your coffee grinder)*

Frozen or fresh fruit

*(I use a few strawberries, peaches, raspberries,
    blackberries, and blueberries)*

Ice (optional but makes it thicker and colder)

Chocolate Banana Smoothie

Blend until smooth.

1 cup of vanilla soymilk, rice milk, or water

1 scoop of Dutch Chocolate Juice Plus+ Complete®
  (See Resource Guide to Order)

1 ripe banana

1 Tablespoon brewer's yeast or nutritional yeast

1 Tablespoon ground flax seed for omega 3's (just put
  whole seeds in your coffee grinder)

1 cup of ice

Jenna's Favorite Parfait

Start with a pretty, long-stemmed glass. Layer the following ingredients. You can make it the night before if you prefer granola that is not too crunchy. Top it with a whole strawberry or design of berries. Pick a pattern and then repeat.

Strawberries, blueberries, or pineapple (any fresh or
  thawed frozen fruit will work)

Granola (organic if possible)

Organic yogurt or non-dairy yogurt

Dried dates or raisins

Wrap-ups to go

This is a great way to get several veggies in at once. Easy to pack and carry. Put it next to a cold or frozen water bottle to keep it cool for several hours.

Whole Wheat Tortillas or Flatbread
Filling: Choice of hummus, beans, organic turkey,
   wild salmon, or other healthy choice
Shredded carrots, purple cabbage, cucumbers, spinach,
   spouts, red peppers, corn or any other veggies
Healthy salad dressing (optional)

Dance Bag Trail Mix
(Place in a small zip-lock snack bag/make enough for the whole week)
5 or 6 raw almonds
5 or 6 raw walnuts
3 Brazil nuts
¼ cup Dried apricots
¼ cup Dried plums
Frosted Mini-Wheat Cereal® (About 8 pieces)

Tips For Eating Out And Choosing Wisely

• Choose foods that are broiled instead of fried, such as a grilled chicken sandwich instead of fried chicken or chicken nuggets, grilled fish instead of fried fish, etc.

• Choose soups that are broth or tomato-based and not cream-based.

• Choose tomato-based sauce instead of Alfredo or cream sauce for pasta. If they have whole-wheat pasta, ask for this as a substitute.

- ALWAYS ask for your salad dressing on the side. Have low-fat salad dressings instead of the "full-fat" kind. Romaine, leaf lettuce or spinach are much more nutritious than iceberg lettuce.

- Always substitute another side dish for French fries. Most restaurants will bring you broccoli or the veggie of the day. Some offer fruit or a salad as a choice. Baked potatoes or sweet potatoes without the butter or sour cream (or with a tiny amount) are better than fries.

- Use mustard or ketchup instead of mayonnaise.

- When ordering a sub or sandwich, select the veggie choice, or leaner meats like turkey or grilled chicken. Stay away from fried items, like burgers or steak and cheese sandwiches.

- Choose water instead of sodas, fruit drinks, and milkshakes.

- When ordering pizza, add lots of veggies instead of meats. Ask for half the cheese or no cheese.

- When ordering Chinese or Asian food, ask for no MSG and ask for veggies to be steamed with the sauce on the side to decrease the fat. Avoid fried foods. Ask for brown rice if available.

• If fruit and veggies are available, try to add them into your meal. For example, have lettuce and tomato on sandwiches or burgers.

Some Ideas for Popular Restaurants

Burger King®, Fuddruckers®, and Backyard Burger®, as well as other restaurants, offer a veggie burger. You owe it to yourself to be brave and try it with lettuce, tomato, onion, ketchup and mustard.

At our local Mexican restaurant I have them make a naked burrito in a bowl with cilantro rice, black beans, pinto beans, lots of chunky salsa and lots of lettuce. This is a delicious vegetarian meal with plenty of plant-based protein.

At Italian restaurants (Macaroni Grill® and Nothing but Noodles® are the ones we have), I order whole wheat pasta with marinara sauce. I add broccoli, carrots, sun dried tomatoes and mushrooms. Delicious!

Some of my best meals have been when I ask the waiter for a plate of their best vegetables. The chefs seem to really like this and they send a beautiful plate every time!

A broth or tomato-based soup with bread is always a good choice.

Almost every restaurant has a grilled or blackened salmon choice. Ask for vegetables and a baked potato to eat with it.

If You Have to Eat Fast Food

You can check out your favorite fast food place or restaurant on the Internet. You can find the company Web site by doing a Google search. Once you have found the Web site, look for the "nutrition section." There is usually a link on the home page to the nutrition section where you will find nutrition facts, including fat, cholesterol, sodium, protein, calories, and more. This will help you make better choices when eating out. Here are a few examples of poor choices and somewhat better choices when you have to eat fast food. You will see that even the "better" choices have huge amounts of sodium and very few nutrients. Try to limit fast food to once a week at the most.

McDonald's® Poor Choices:

Small fries (250 calories; 13 g fat; 140 mg sodium)
Large fries (570 calories; 30 g fat; 330 mg sodium)
Quarter-pounder with cheese (510 calories; 26 g fat; 1190 mg sodium)
Nuggets 6-pack (250 calories; 15 g fat; 670 mg sodium)
Strawberry triple-thick shake (1110 calories; 27 g fat; 130 mg sodium)

McDonald's® Better Choices
Fruit and yogurt parfait (180 calories; 2 g fat; 85 mg sodium)
Southwest salad with grilled chicken (320 calories; 9 g fat;
970 mg sodium)

Chick-fil-A® Poor Choices:
Chicken biscuit (420 calories; 19 g fat; 1270 mg sodium)
Chicken sandwich (410 calories; 16 g fat; 1300 mg sodium)

Chick-fil-A® Better Choices
Char-grilled sandwich (ask for lettuce and tomato; 270 calories;
3.5 g fat; 940 mg sodium)
Char-grilled salad (this is without dressing/choose low fat or
non-fat; 180 calories; 6 g fat; 620 mg sodium)

Taco Bell® Poor Choices
Grilled Beef Burrito (680 calories; 30 g fat; 2120 mg sodium)
Fiesta Taco Salad (840 calories; 45 g fat; 1780 mg sodium)
(without shell; 470 calories; 25 g fat; 1510 mg sodium)

Taco Bell® Better Choices
Crunchy Tacos (150 calories; 8 g fat; 370 mg sodium)
Grilled Steak Soft Shell (160 calories; 4.5 g fat; 550 mg sodium)
Spicy Chicken Soft Taco (170 calories; 6 g fat; 580 mg sodium)

Wendy's® Poor Choices
Big Bacon Classic Sandwich (590 calories; 30 g fat; 1510 mg
sodium)

Chicken Club Sandwich (650 calories; 31 g fat; 1580 mg sodium)
Medium Chocolate Frosty (430 calories; 55 g sugar)

Wendy's® Better Choices
Sour Cream and Chives Baked Potato (320 calories; 4 g fat;
  55 mg sodium)
Mandarin Chicken Salad (170 calories; 2 g fat; 480 mg sodium;
  add dressing: 190 calories)
Caesar Chicken Salad (90 calories; 5 g fat; 620 mg sodium; add
  dressing: 120 calories)

Burger King® Poor Choices
Double Whopper® w/cheese (990 calories; 64 g fat; 1520 mg
  sodium)
Spicy Chicken Sandwich (720 calories; 36 g fat; 2000 mg
  sodium)
Onion Rings—Large (450 calories; 22 g fat; 660 mg sodium)

Burger King® Better Choices
Chicken Garden Salad (240 calories; 9 g fat; 720 mg sodium; add
  light Italian dressing: 120 calories; 11 g fat; 440 mg sodium
Chicken Tenders, 5 pc. (210 calories; 12 g fat; 600 mg sodium)

Grocery Shopping—Be A Smart Shopper

• Try to buy foods that contain ingredients that you
  recognize or would use at home (if you can't pronounce
  it...use caution).

- Stay on the perimeter of the grocery store. This is where the fresh, whole food is sold. Even better, visit your local farmer's market for vine-ripened fresh fruits and vegetables.

> Dancers need to ingest sufficient energy to meet the physical demands of their intense and oftentimes lengthy training sessions. Consuming the right amounts and types of food and fluid will provide their body with the fuel needed to achieve optimal training benefits and peak performance.
>
> —Tina Marie Mendieta MS, RD/LDN

- Avoid products containing the following ingredients: trans fats, partially hydrogenated oils, artificial sweeteners (aspartame or Splenda®), MSG, nitrites, nitrates, artificial colors, sulfites, potassium bromate, and brominated vegetable oil.

- The following terms all mean one thing—sugar— brown sugar, honey, dextrose, maltose, lactose, fructose, rock sugar, and corn syrup and high-fructose corn syrup. No one sugar is healthier or better than another, they are all simply empty calories and replace healthier choices. High sugar in your diet will depress your immune system and compromise your health.

- Check serving sizes. Most of us eat much more than a

typical serving. A small bag of chips might actually be
2½ servings. This is a sneaky trick. You must multiply the
calories and fat by the number of servings or by 2.5 in this
case to get your total intake.

What is a serving size?

It is more important to eat a variety of fruits and vegetables
of many colors than to worry about the exact serving size.
Most foods are ½ cup per serving. Loose foods like lettuce
are one cup and dried fruit and nuts (denser foods) are ¼
cup. Dancers often need more calories than less active people
but the extra servings should still come from healthy sources.

Foods That Drain the Body and Brain

The list of these foods is long: white bread, white sugar,
alcohol, artificial sweeteners, artificial food colorings, colas,
frostings, corn syrup, nitrate and nitrate-containing foods,
high sugar drinks, candy, nicotine, processed snacks, fast
food with high fat and sodium, and any foods with a long
list of ingredients you don't recognize as real foods.

Extreme Super Foods for Serious Dancers—Choose Some to Eat Every Day!!!!

Nutrition-packed food choices will improve your
performance and help to prevent illness now and when you

are older. Research is showing that these foods truly can make a difference:

wild salmon, beans, walnuts, avocados, Brazil nuts, spinach, blueberries, sweet potatoes, broccoli, cinnamon, garlic, kiwi, collard greens, kale, brown rice, bananas, soy, oranges, onions, dried fruit (apricots, figs, plums, raisins, dates, cranberries), tomatoes, black and green tea, and pumpkin.

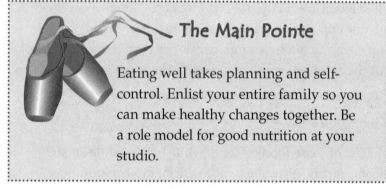

The Main Pointe

Eating well takes planning and self-control. Enlist your entire family so you can make healthy changes together. Be a role model for good nutrition at your studio.

12. Hydration and Fluid Intake

Everyone, including dancers, should drink 6 to 8 glasses (8 ounces) of water each day. Children should consume half of their weight in ounces. A 50 lb child would need 25 ounces per day. Adequate fluid intake is necessary to replace fluids lost through metabolism, daily activity, dance class, and other vigorous exercise. The amount lost depends on many factors including environmental temperature, humidity, and your ability to dissipate heat. When you are dehydrated, even just a little, studies have shown that your energy level will drop as well as your ability to focus. Every system in your body depends on water to work properly.

Many popular sports drinks are high in sugar and lack many nutrients, making them essentially empty calories. The body does not hydrate efficiently with substances other than water, which should be the first-choice beverage for an athlete. Electrolytes, which are found in many sports drinks, are easily obtained with the proper diet.

—Pamela A. Popper, PhD, ND,
From *The Wellness Forum's Guide to Sports Nutrition*

Drink water before, during and after your class. Foods like bananas, oranges, and kiwis will help you keep the electrolytes that you need for long workouts. Sports drinks with high sugar content can cause cramping and are not recommended. A drink like Propel®, with a tiny bit of carbohydrate may improve taste and help dancers consume more fluid. Do not choose drinks with chemical and artificial sweeteners like Nutrasweet® or Splenda®.

Guidelines for Exercise—Fluid Replacement

• Consume 8 to 16 ounces of fluid at least one hour before the start of dance.

• Consume 4 to 8 ounces of fluid every 10 to 15 minutes during the workout.

• Consume 16 to 24 ounces during the 30 minutes after exercise even if you do not feel thirsty.

What's the Big Deal about Soft Drinks?
Dancers have no reason to consume regular or diet sodas. They can only hurt performance and decrease health.

• High sugar content (23 g for 8 ounces/which is about 6 teaspoons for every 8 ounces)

• No nutrients (we call these "empty" or "liquid calories")

• High phosphorous, which
depletes calcium from bones,
teeth and blood

• Replaces healthy choices like
water

• Diet drinks have aspartame
and Splenda® (chemicals)

• Caffeine (addictive, depletes bones)

Ten Ways to Add More Water to Your Day

1. Always carry a bottle of water with you in the car. Drink on the way to your destination and on the way home.

2. Ice it down. Cold water tastes better.

3. Set a goal. For adults, fill two 32-ounce containers in the morning and make a goal to finish them before bedtime. Young dancers should drink half their weight in ounces.

4. Ask your teachers if you can keep a bottle of water on your desk at school to sip all day. Your brain is 85% water and cannot function or focus without proper hydration.

5. Drink with a straw. It goes down faster and easier.

6. Squeeze in lemon, lime, or orange juice to add a bit of flavor.

7. Humans sometimes mistake thirst for hunger. When you are hungry start with a glass of water.

8. Eat fruits and vegetables that contain a lot of water, such as watermelon, oranges, celery, carrots, and lettuce.

9. Next time you start to order a soda, stop and get water with lemon. You have just saved yourself 10 teaspoons of sugar or more. Your body will thank you.

10. Be a role model at dance class and at competitions. Make sure all the other kids see you drink water instead of sodas or sugary drinks.

The Main Pointe

Water is necessary for every function in your body. Humans have a faulty thirst mechanism so you have to take purposeful water breaks and make a plan to stay hydrated before, during and after training or performing.

13. Body Image and Disordered Eating

—with Charee Boulter, PhD, Psychologist

Adolescence is a time when many changes are happening to your body. As you mature, your body begins to transform from the body of child to a more adult body. During this time questions about your appearance are common. Additionally, there is considerable pressure to have the "right look" that is promoted in magazines, on TV and in the movies.

For a dancer, the awareness of physical changes in appearance and in the body's ability to adapt to the changes can be heightened. How your body feels during different movements also changes. Dance moves that once were easy may be more difficult during a growth spurt. Because dancers have more muscle, you might weigh more than your friends who are the same size. As a dancer you may find that your awareness of these physical changes is amplified because you spend several hours per week in front of a mirror wearing a leotard.

Individual feelings of self-doubt and self-consciousness can lead a dancer to criticize her body. Comments from your dance instructor on body position, which are intended to help you improve your form and skills, can sound harsh and critical. On a day when you are feeling low, comments such as, "raise your leg higher," may sound like criticisms of your body. Thus, "raise your leg higher" may become interpreted as "my legs are too short" or "my legs are too big."

Sometimes when a dancer struggles with body image concerns she may begin to diet in an attempt to change her body shape. It is important to remember that healthy nutrition is key to optimal functioning as a dancer. Diets often eliminate crucial nutrients and/or adequate calories thus placing a dancer at risk for a variety of physical problems (exhaustion, weakness, stress fractures, etc.). When diets go awry, disordered eating can be the result.

An eating disorder is complex and is much more than a body image disturbance combined with an out-of-control diet. There are many factors related to the development of an eating disorder. A dancer is not "crazy" if she develops an eating disorder. In fact some of the personal attributes that help a dancer excel can also place her at risk of developing an eating disorder, such as high achieving, being overly goal-directed, and paying attention to detail. Some dancers may appear confident but may actually struggle with low self-esteem. Some may have a family history of eating disorders or other mental health disorders that place them at increased risk.

An eating disorder can have significant negative effects on one's health. The most serious is death. In 1997, Heidi Guenther, a professional ballet dancer, died due to health complications related to an eating disorder. Problems that may be of heightened concern for dancers include:

• Fatigue

• Dizziness

• Decreased ability to concentrate

• Increased overuse injuries

• Stress fractures

• Decreased cardiac functioning (increased risk of heart failure)

• Weakened immune system

You may be concerned that you or a friend may be struggling with body image concerns, but are not sure. Check the list below to help you determine if it may be a serious body image problem or just run of the mill self doubts.

Signs of body image dissatisfaction

• Do you frequently make negative comments about yourself?

• Do you avoid shopping for clothes with others (especially trying on clothes in common dressing rooms)?

• Do you often ask others about your appearance—"Does this look OK?"

• Do you frequently have "bad hair" days?

• Do you notice that you get into bad moods connected to your feelings about appearance and/or weight?

• Do you often notice or comment upon the appearance of others—both positive and negative?

• Do you often compare yourself to others—"She is so pretty and I'm not. Her life is perfect."

• Do your thoughts and worries about your appearance interfere with your daily activities?

• Do you worry so much about how you look that it is difficult to concentrate and learn the choreography in class?

• Does getting dressed take too long due to multiple clothing changes?

• Noticeable weight changes in a short period of time

• Excessive dieting, even after achieving original goal.

• Belief that one is fat even though she is not.

• Changes in eating patterns—ex: eating alone, eating limited types of food.

• Avoiding social events where food is served.

• Uncontrolled binge eating.

• Use of dieting, purging, exercise or medications to compensate for overeating.

• Mood is dependent upon weight.

• Absence of menstrual periods.

What should you do if you have a friend struggling with body image issues? It is important to know the common signs of an eating disorder. If you recognize these signs in yourself or a friend, please talk to a trusted adult and seek professional assistance.

Help is available for dancers struggling with disordered eating. Comprehensive treatment usually involves medical care, individual and group therapy, and nutritional therapy. A treatment team, which may include a physician, a therapist, and a dietitian, is often convened to address the dancer holistically. In some cases the dance instructor may be included in some aspects of the team, for example, if the dancer needs to take some time away from dance during recovery. Family therapy may be a component of treatment. In most cases, outpatient treatment is sufficient. Some individuals may need more intensive care and thus, may spend time in a hospital or inpatient treatment center.

What to say to a friend struggling with body image issues

• Make positive comments about her personality and talents.

• If she makes negative self-comments, tell her that you feel sad when she says such things about herself.

• Reassure her that she is beautiful inside and out.

• Avoid making comments about your physical appearance and others.

• Make an effort to focus on the strengths and functions of the body rather than the appearance of one's body.

If you suspect that a friend is struggling with an eating disorder, talk to her. Tell her that you are concerned and offer to go with her to see a school counselor, trusted teacher or a health professional.

She may be embarrassed and try to hide her disorder, so do not worry if she does not seem happy that you are expressing your concern.

- Find a time when you are not likely to be interrupted.

- Use "I" messages to identify your concern and avoid accusing her of having a problem:

- "I am worried about you."

- Tell her what you are worried about.

- Identify specific concerns such as: noticeable changes in eating patterns, physical fatigue, negative body image, etc.

- "I have noticed you seem really tired and you have been dieting. I am concerned that you might have an eating disorder."

- Be a good listener.

- She might open up and share her struggles with you.

- She might deny having a problem. You can be a good friend and listen.

- Be understanding.

• Remember that having an eating disorder does not make a person crazy.

• You can probably relate to some of her feelings and concerns, but to a lesser degree.

• Ask her to see a professional.

If your friend is not at a point where they are willing to seek help, confide in a trusted adult, perhaps your dance teacher or a parent. You can also talk to a counselor who specializes in eating disorders to get advice. This is not something that you can fix for your friend. They need professional help.

Treatment for an eating disorder can be lengthy. Sometimes a dancer may begin to make improvements by addressing the underlying issues—family issues, depressed mood, low self-esteem—before the eating behaviors improve. Be patient. The end result of successful treatment is worth it.

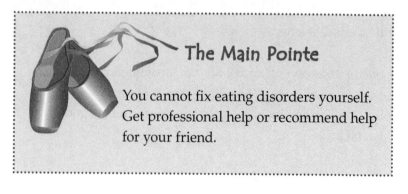

The Main Pointe

You cannot fix eating disorders yourself. Get professional help or recommend help for your friend.

14. Attending Dance Conventions

—with Jenna Lee Branner

Dance conventions, master classes and intensive study programs are excellent ways to improve your skills, become more versatile, and learn from great teachers and choreographers. This is a chance to dance for the sake of dancing. The ability to learn or "pick up" combinations quickly is a skill you will improve in this environment. You may attend with your studio or dance company or you may sign up and go as an individual. Some are on weekends and some are entire weeks during the summer or holiday vacations. Many summer intensives require an audition either in person or by sending in a video of your performance. If your goal is to dance professionally, conventions are a great way to get to know the styles of working choreographers and for them to see you dance.

How to Pack for a Convention

- Water bottle or cooler of drinks (sometimes you only have a few seconds between classes, so don't count on waiting in line at the water fountain or the water table)

Lots of "10-second snacks"
- Baggies of whole-grain cereal with dried fruit

Style is all about individuality. If you don't feel empowered by what you're wearing there is no way you will pull it off. You have to believe fully in the look you're trying to achieve. Personal style can be derived from other trends that you see. If you like something, take it, put a twist on it, and make it your own. My advice to all dancers trying to make it in the hip-hop scene is... STAY AWAY FROM TIGHT CLOTHES! It just looks terrible. You've got to get something that makes you feel less pulled up. You simply have to dress the part, and eventually the dancing will catch up.

—Brian Friedman, Teacher, Professional Dancer, Judge and Choreographer for "So You Think You Can Dance" TV Show, Dance Shoe and Clothing Designer

- Fruit of any kind—orange slices, apples—fresh pineapple has an enzyme that repairs muscle

- Raw almonds and walnuts mixed with dried fruit

- Healthy sports bars/granola bars are preferable to fast food or vending machines (try Kashi® brand or a bar with low sugar, high-fiber, and a plant-based protein source)

- Homemade banana bread or muffins

- Whole-grain bagel with peanut butter

A plan for lunch

• Bring either a lunch packed in a bag, or have a cell phone, so someone can bring food to you

Ideas for Packing a Lunch at Convention Time

• Sandwich with hummus, spreadable fruit and peanut or almond butter, organic turkey

• Tortilla wrap with veggies, beans and avocados

• Pita pocket with veggies, tuna, hummus, etc.

First aid items such as Band-Aids, toe tape, ankle or knee brace if you use one

• Toiletries and hair supplies: deodorant, hairbrush, hairspray, bobby pins, ponytail holders, barrettes

• All types of dance shoes—jazz, tap, ballet, foot paws, sneakers for hip-hop

• Socks—many conventions are held in carpeted ballrooms. Socks work well on the carpet and prevent carpet burns if you cannot get a spot on the small wooden dance floor.

What Do I Wear??????

Believe it or not, the first impression you make on a teacher or choreographer is very important. Dressing specifically for each style of dance can help you feel comfortable and look the part. Don't worry if your duffle bag is overflowing. Wear a dance bra and shorts for your base and then you can add clothes quickly in the break between classes.

Jazz Class
Wear something that flatters your body type. Wear your hair partly down or in a ponytail.

Yes	No
Booty shorts	Ballet tights
Bra tops	Leotard
Jazz pants	Baggy pants/shorts
Tank tops	T-shirts

Lyrical or Contemporary Class
Some people wear their hair down and flowing for lyrical class. Wear something that reflects your style or the style of the teacher.

Yes	No
Long sleeve T-shirt	Ballet tights
Loose or tight shorts	Leotard
Capri tights or sweatpants	Hair in a bun

Hip-hop Class

Street clothes that you can move in are the best. Do not wear ballet or jazz shoes and definitely do not go barefoot. Never wear your hair in a bun to hip-hop class. This is where you can really express your individual style.

Yes	No
Sneakers	Jazz sneakers
Long sleeve shirt	Tight shirt
Baggy shorts	Leotard and tights
Sweat pants or jeans	Tight shorts or pants
Hats	Bare feet
Jacket or Hooded Sweatshirt	
Accessories (bandana or scarf)	

Ballet Class

Traditionally, all students wear pink tights, black leotards, and ballet or pointe shoes. Hair must be in a tight bun with no loose strands. Many times at dance conventions, this dress code is relaxed due to limited changing time between classes.

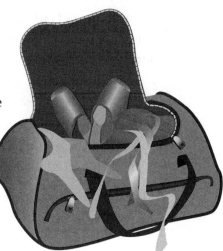

Tap Class
It is easy to forget your tap shoes for conventions, so check the schedule to see if a tap class will be taught. There are no rules for clothing, so just be comfortable. If you are not a tapper, put on your sneakers and try your best. Sitting out is considered disrespectful to the teachers at the convention. By joining in, you will get a taste for the intricacy and difficulty involved in performing tap.

Dance Etiquette

• Don't be late. In most classes, ballet especially, it is better not to come at all than to disrupt the class.

• Try not to yawn. Even if you are going on your fifth hour of class that night and suffering from a severe case of sleep deprivation, try to resist the urge. If you absolutely have to, make sure you cover your mouth.

• Don't chew gum. Enough said.

Tap Dancing is not like riding a bike.
Consistency and hard work are key.

—Jason Janas, Professional Dancer, Teacher, Choreographer,
Owner of Hoofin' Ground Inc.

- Be courteous to other dancers. Try to control yourself. If you find that you are bumping into people constantly and occasionally knocking someone's teeth out with your battement, I would suggest you stand in the back corner. Also if you are tall enough to be a Rockette, it is best to stand toward the back so other shorter dancers can get a chance to see the teacher or choreographer.

- Be respectful to the teacher. Do not get in the front if you do not know the combination well or if you are not a "regular" in the classes. Don't ever sit down or cross your arms. Always make sure you thank the teacher at the end, and in most classes, it is expected that the group applaud at the end as well.

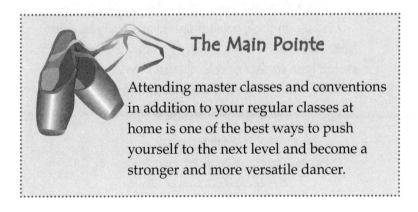

The Main Pointe

Attending master classes and conventions in addition to your regular classes at home is one of the best ways to push yourself to the next level and become a stronger and more versatile dancer.

I would love to tell dancers to dance from the heart. Let people see inside of you when you dance. This letting in can be achieved through using your eyes. Make sure that there is a light in your eyes that the audience can see, which allows the audience into your soul and into the essence of what you feel when you dance.

I would also tell dancers to practice full out every time. Your body remembers how it practices and this translates to the stage. Practice full out and your body will only know full out when it hits the stage.

Dancers who want to be professional need to learn professionalism at a young age. This would include: showing up on time, being prepared and ready to work hard. There aren't many days off if you are a working dancer. Push to that next level even if you don't think you can. When you push you will find that you really will make it to the next level.

—Edith Montoya
Owner and Director of Dance Precisions in Placentia, CA,
Owner of Elite Designs Costuming

15. Time Management for Dancers

—*with Jenna Lee Branner*

S o here's the scenario: you have just walked in the door from dance. It is 10:30 p.m. and you have not been home since that morning when you left for school. This means you probably have to eat, shower, unpack and repack for the next day, do all your homework, and oh yeah, sleep. Here are some tips to keep the stress level to a minimum.

As soon as you get home, get whoever is still awake to fix you something healthy to eat or just fix it yourself. As you learned in the nutrition chapter, it is important to replace the glycogen in your muscles within 30 minutes after your workout. Ignore the rumor that you shouldn't eat anything later in the evening because the truth is your tired body needs to replenish itself no matter what time it is.

Assess the homework situation and make a plan. Get your priorities straight and work on the hardest assignments or the ones that matter the most first. It's best that you work on your homework in a semi-uncomfortable place - nowhere near a bed, couch, or pillow. You associate all those things with sleep and you will be tempted to go to sleep right away. If you start nodding off or if your eyelids feel like they weigh 50 pounds each, it is time to call it a night. Your brain will function better on some sleep even if it's not a lot. So set your alarm for as early as you need to, to get up and make sure you have enough time to accomplish everything. Maybe set two or three alarms!

When you are at school make use of little pockets of free time to do your homework for the next day, gather research materials, and get extra help from your teachers. Ask for the next week's assignments on Friday so you can get ahead on the weekends. Make sure your teachers know what your schedule is like so if you look sleepy in class, they won't take it personally.

Having a boyfriend is difficult when you dance. You have very little time for dates or talking on the phone. This is one thing my parents like about my busy schedule!

Take a shower. Use this as a time to plan out how much you have to do and how you are going to get it all done. Make a schedule in your mind for yourself while your body is relaxing.

Hint: If you have vocabulary words or something to memorize and your shower door is clear glass, then tape the sheet of paper onto the door from the outside so it is facing in. Your schoolwork won't get wet and you won't fall asleep studying. Plus it is a brand new study spot and helps you learn the material better.

Don't waste time. Turn off your computer so MySpace and Facebook don't use their addictive powers on you. Turn off the sound alarm that tells you when a new e-mail arrives. This will distract you from your work. Allow yourself 10 minutes to check e-mail and other computer messages and then resist the urge. Remember the faster you get your work done, the more sleep you get.

If you cannot stop interruptions then go to another room or to the library when you need time alone. Fight for your right to work without distractions.

Divide the items on your to-do list into Urgent and Non-Urgent, or sometimes I use A-B-C to prioritize. As are things I have to do tonight, Bs would be great to finish but I could also work on them tomorrow, and Cs are things I wish I had time to do but they might have to wait for the weekend. You can use colored markers to prioritize right in your planner while at school.

Break really big projects into smaller chunks of work. On your list, mark off the parts of the project as you finish each one.

Organize your workspace so you can find paper, pencils, note cards, calculator, and reference books quickly and without wasting time.

If you have appointments or breaks in your dance schedule, always have reading material or notes to study. Little pockets of time can really add up.

Know yourself. If you know you can't resist looking at your cell phone every two minutes to see your text messages and missed calls—leave it in the laundry room or the garage until your work is finished. If you know you work better after a snack, then take time to eat and then get to work. Are you a morning person or a night owl? Do you like to study in groups or by yourself? The more you know about yourself the more efficient and effective you can be.

When your parents see your good grades they will be much more supportive of your dance commitments.

The Main Pointe

Spend your precious time on things that truly are important and make a difference. Good grades, becoming a better dancer, getting enough sleep, and spending time with your family or a friend are all worthwhile and will have a lasting benefit. Watching TV, instant messaging and surfing the Internet may have to wait.

16. Surviving and Thriving as a Dance Family

—with Will Branner and William Branner, MD

Mom, Dad, and a Section for Cool Brothers and Sisters

Being a father of a dancer means more than sitting in a dark auditorium waiting for your child to perform. Fortunately for us, the expectations for you as a Dance Dad are not too high but there are basic rules you must understand and follow. Obviously, the rules will differ slightly depending on whether your child is performing at a recital, a concert, or a three-day regional dance competition. Hopefully you will discover this after only one or two events. The obvious ones, such as arrive early and wear comfortable clothes in layers, are similar to what you would find in any college entrance exam prep book. This chapter will prepare you for the many other rules that require more experience and preparation. So don't be nervous.

Arrive early because you will have to drop off your dancer to allow her to be ready by her call time, which usually is one to two hours before she is scheduled to perform. You will be unloading props and boxes of costumes, shoes and make-up, too. This will take more time than you think. You will also have other family members with you who will be working as a team to get the best seats possible. Since there are no reserved seats and saving seats is frowned upon, their mission is critical. You will have to count on your group to save you a seat while you go find a place to park the car and hike all the way back to the auditorium.

Make sure you wear your dance studio's logo or color somewhere on your body. Bring a noisemaker, like an empty plastic water bottle with a few small rocks or beads slipped inside. And definitely spring for the competition program or you will be lost. This program lists all the competition numbers under the category in which they will compete, and from this, you can estimate the approximate time your dancer and her friends will compete. Be aware though, the numbers sometime go out of order and each routine is only about three minutes long. You certainly don't want to be

caught in line at the concession stand or be standing in the men's bathroom when your number is called and you miss your dancer's routine. If you do miss it, definitely don't admit to it. Nothing could be worse. Smile, give her hug and tell her she showed great energy this time. Maybe she won't find out.

Choose your seat quickly and with confidence—dance parents can be an assertive bunch. Any hesitation on your part will be interpreted by the Dance Moms as a sign of weakness. Your group should have selected seats in an area with other parents from your studio, hopefully a row or two behind the dance teacher and as close to your child's peers as possible. Doing so will allow you to experience the event and see the excitement through your child's eyes and will definitely make it more fun.

Don't "boo" the performers competing against your child. As much as you might want to turn this into a hockey game, a polite clap is better. Since the judges may be influenced by the loudness of the applause, a noiseless clap for the competition is best. No reason to help out the other team, right? But it is OK to yell and clap loudly when your group takes the stage–the louder the better. The kids really do perform better if they sense any excitement from the audience. Generally any sounds you might have made at a wrestling match or NASCAR event would do well here.

Enjoy the concessions. Many of the competition venues have an excellent selection of sandwiches, ice cream and specialty drinks but few healthy choices so if you are inclined to eat when you're bored, be careful. Consider having a nearby pizza store deliver a large order but you may have to eat it on the steps because some places absolutely do not allow outside food to be brought into the auditorium. I have found a six-inch sub sandwich slips nicely into a coat pocket and if you go easy on the onions no one will ever know.

Bring a survival kit. Competition auditoriums are inherently dark, cold and noisy places–think camping in a cavern–there will be blocks of time with nothing happening onstage that you need to see, so you will need to bring a few things:

- A blanket and pillow: it is possible to snooze a little in your seat and with practice you will find a position that works well enough. Left foot on the seat in front, right foot on the floor, hands clasped under my chin and right elbow on the armrest works well for me.

- Earplugs: the music is usually excellent quality but is loud and relentless. Some seats with good views of the stage are close to the speakers. At least one of the competition emcees has an especially loud and shrill voice, which she loves to show off at award ceremonies. If you don't have earplugs, two balled-up pieces of napkin work well.

- Something to read or work on: a laptop computer, video games or just a newspaper will help fill the time between the dances you want to see.

- Cash: your experience as a human ATM will come in handy here.

Forget about sneaking away for golf or to a nearby sports bar to catch the semifinals of the NCAA basketball tournament. This is March Madness of a different sort.

My children's studio, Weir Dancin', in Matthews, North Carolina, has over 75 competitive dancers, each competing in various solo, duet/trio, small group, and large group categories subdivided into jazz, tap, lyrical, hip-hop, and musical theatre numbers which are further subdivided by age groups. Each year we enter a weeklong competition, (it's called "Nationals") which draws studios from several surrounding states. Last year there were 1,339 separate competitive numbers at Nationals and our studio's 116 numbers were spread pretty evenly throughout the week. You do the math. Just to see our entire studio's numbers required over five and half hours of sitting in my seat. Add in numbers from other studios that were worth seeing as well as the numbers that preceded or followed the dances you want to see and you easily triple that number. Spending over 15 hours in a week watching dancing leaves very little time for anything else.

To sing well and to dance is to be well educated.

—Plato

Get an experienced Dance Mom to explain the awards system to you. It is complicated. At times it reads like the IRS tax code. They differ at each event but the basic idea is every number gets a score and an award. It's not like the Olympics. Silver is bad, Gold is pretty good, but Platinum is the one everyone hopes to get. And just because your child got a

Platinum Award doesn't mean he or she won. A range of point scores qualifies as Platinum, for example, and although Platinum scores are seldom given out, a higher Platinum score might have beaten your child.

Familiarize yourself with the dance moves. Most have French names. A fouetté is a turn characterized by a whipping action of the foot or leg out to an open position and quickly back in again, a jeté is a leap, and a grand jeté is a big leap. Do not try these yourself, especially the fouetté. These take months of practice to perfect. You will see port de bras, arabesques, and pirouettes, and with experience, you will actually be able to tell a good one from a bad one. Look for sharp arm movements, high kicks, changes in facial expressions, and "ballet" hands. You will understand that when Taylor did 17 second-turns in a row it was truly amazing. You will gain confidence enough to say one day, "Jenna really nailed her turn section and her grand jetés were strong" and truly mean it. And it won't bother you when the Dance Moms laugh at your comments because you know they are secretly very impressed.

As a father of a dancer, your number one role is support. Get involved. Be a prop dad. Take pictures of everyone's kids. Put together a first aid kit and become the one the kids come to for a bandage or icepack. You can be confident that the money you spend on dance is being put to good use. The dance world is teaching your child life skills and confidence.

These performers become athletes. They train and practice as much or more than football players. They put their hearts into each performance. With these guidelines and a little effort, you will survive and thrive at their recitals, rehearsals, concerts, and competitions. And, just you being there will make all the difference in the world.

—*Billy Branner, Jenna's Dad*

Brother and Sister Survival Guide

—*Will Branner, Jenna's Brother*

**Ten Ways to Entertain Yourself
at a Three-Day Dance Competition**

If you are under 12 years old

1. Bring action figures and toy cars

2. Make a fort out of the seats and your parent's blankets

3. Draw funny faces and mustaches on the people in the program

4. Bring a football to throw outside with your Dad between dances

5. Eat something from the concession stand every hour (get money from Mom or Dad)

6. Bring your Game Boy

7. Bring your portable DVD player to watch a movie

8. Take a nap on the far aisle by the wall

9. Watch your sister (or brother) dance

10. Tell her/him how great she/he did!

If you are over 12 years old

1. Bring a watch or cell phone so you can keep track of when your sister or brother dances again

2. Bring an I-pod or another way to listen to your own music

3. Meet girls and kids from other studios

4. Bring homework and get ahead for the coming week

5. Meet more girls

6. Bring your portable gaming system (remember to charge it before you leave home)

7. Take a nap by propping your elbow on the armrest

8. Meet even more girls

9. Actually watch most of the dances. You will be impressed.

10. If you can't beat them—join them!!!! (After six years of attending recitals and competitions as Jenna's brother, I joined the hip-hop team at our studio. Now I have even more fun as part of the team.)

Notes from a Dance Mom

The happiest dance moms are the ones who embrace and enjoy every minute of their child's dance career. Jenna has one more year of competition dancing and I am having trouble imagining life without costumes, travel, long hours of sitting in an auditorium seat and yes - even the bills! I can't think of anything more rewarding than being a witness to the planning, amazing choreography sessions, and hard work that go into creating a dance number and then seeing it come to fruition on the stage. As you watch all of the dancers, the advanced and the beginners, one thing stands out—these kids all love to dance. Most of them couldn't care less which award they receive. They love the atmosphere, the social time with friends, and the chance to shine with lights and video cameras rolling. They are also very interested in pleasing their teachers and doing justice to the choreography.

If your child is in a ballet company, the audience is politely enthusiastic with proper theatre etiquette. If your child performs in competition dance, the support is more vocal and loud. Our team puts beans in empty water bottles to shake and we cheer when our group comes onstage. We have cowbells and shakers. The more we cheer the better the kids dance. The juniors support the seniors and vice versa and we have families that come early and stay late just to be there to cheer for their fellow dancers.

Here are some practical "Mom" tips that may save you from learning things the hard way

Have a family meeting to decide how much time and money can be devoted to dance. If one parent is hiding bills and secretly panicked over the costume payment it will add stress to the family. Usually there are fund-raising opportunities to help defray the cost, or maybe priorities can be reset to shift funds to dance payments. It can be a very expensive sport.

Make time to "hang out" at the studio. Usually the last few minutes of a class the doors are left open and we can peak in to see the results of hours of hard work. Our studio allows parents to watch during solo and duet/trio practice. I love to be a fly on the wall as our genius (truly they are) teachers create new pieces. I love to watch the kid's progress from the beginnings of a dance in October to their amazing performance at Nationals the following summer. Skills are learned, leaps and turns improve, and confidence builds. Best of all is seeing them work as a team.

If your studio attends a dance convention, buy an "observer pass" to allow you to go into the ballroom and watch. This may seem expensive (usually $20 to $30) but it is so worth it. Go in for the last 10 minutes of each class. This is when they are performing the combination they have just learned in groups. You will have so much to talk about on the way home when you have watched this portion for each choreographer. Many times the teachers talk to the students about dance and life in general. You will also learn so much about your child and how they learn and respond in a creative (and often crowded) environment. A part of this passion will rub off on you.

My mother enrolled me in tap lessons when I was 5 years old. After a few weeks the dance teacher told my mom to find me another hobby because I had two left feet and would never be a dancer. I loved to tap and wanted to stay in the class, and I did! Now many years later as I have made a successful career in dance, I look back and realized that if you persevere in something you love, you will be successful!

—Shea Sullivan, Faculty at Broadway Dance Center, Choreographer, President of SAS Productions, Inc

Make a detailed list (Jenna's is computerized) of every single costume and accessory so you can check them off as you pack for a competition. We put everything for each dance in a 2-gallon zip lock bag with the name of the dance and all hats, tights, shoes, etc. written with Sharpie® markers on the outside of the bag. Nothing is more stressful than driving two hours to compete only to find you are missing a tap shoe. Dancers under 13 usually need help with packing, but after that, it is their responsibility to make sure they have everything.

Make sure your dancer knows that being able to dance is a privilege. I hear some dancers yelling at their mothers in the dressing room if their hair is not quite right or if they take too long to safety pin a strap. This defeats the positive aspects of the experience and needs to be stopped at all costs. It is supposed to be fun for the whole family. Speak to each other with respect and caring.

It is OK to give your dancer an honest opinion about a performance, such as, "Great energy but a few of the turns were off." They already know if something went wrong so you can be truthful without being critical. I always enjoy watching even if a few things go wrong so I can always honestly say "I loved that number."

Go out of your way to be friendly to the other teams and competition parents. Make friends with any new parents in your company. They usually have questions about how things work. This spirit of hospitality will rub off on your children. Our students make new friends at every competition and congratulate other dancers as they come off stage.

Drive to and from dance as much as possible. We have amazing conversations on these car rides. I was actually very sad when Jenna earned her driver's license, although I am getting more sleep. When she has a very late night we still go to pick her up. She has her whole life to drive herself home!

Try to eat healthy as a family, exercise and manage stress in a proactive way. You must be a great role model for your dancer. Studies show the number one predictor of whether your children will grow up and have healthy habits is whether you model this for them.

Most of all have fun and treasure every moment.

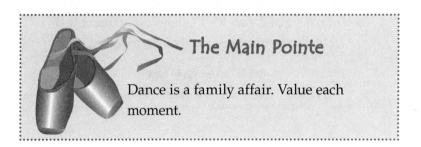

The Main Pointe

Dance is a family affair. Value each moment.

Never did I imagine the person my daughter would become when she became a dancer. Not only has she developed into a talented dancer, she has also learned the invaluable real life skills of time management, organization, commitment and conflict resolution. Competition dance has prepared her for adulthood and has enriched her life in so many ways. If you are the fortunate parents of a dancer just beginning competition dance, the best words of advice are to enjoy every single minute of this wonderful bonding experience. Although there are times when you will question the hectic schedule, dance expenses and occasional bouts of drama, these moments will never compare to the time you are blessed to share while driving to and from dance rehearsals and competitions. You will make many new friendships and you and your dancer will create a sincere personal relationship that will last a lifetime. You always cherish the time you spend together and your dancer will always be grateful for the sacrifices that you have made to support her love of the art of dance. It's a family commitment that can also be cherished family time together.

—Linda Hoverman O'Neal
Real Estate Professional and Mother of Taylor Age 15

17. Lessons for Life

—with Jenna Lee Branner

How Dance Can Prepare You for Future Success and Happiness

Here are some things that I have learned through dance that I believe will help me in life

Dedication—If you are serious about dance, you commit your body, your mind, your time, and your energy to it. I have learned to devote my life to something I truly care about.

Confidence—To make yourself step onto a huge stage with bright lights shining in your eyes, judges in front of you, and an endless audience takes a great deal of confidence. Also, to be criticized and critiqued all the time, while still remaining comfortable in your own skin, takes confidence as well. This self-assurance will help me take new opportunities in the future without hesitation and it will keep me from holding back.

Time Management—I have learned to make use of time. If I have homework or something to do, I get it done efficiently because the faster it gets done, the more sleep I get.

Passion—For me, dance is something that I can turn to for support. I can express myself without having to explain anything. It is an escape for me when everything else is going wrong. Once you have found a passion, it becomes a base that you can always return to even if you are 45 years old and CEO of a company.

Perseverance—Lying on the dance floor, gasping for breath and hurting all over while salty sweat stings my eyes, I hear my teacher say, "From the top!" Sound familiar? Dance has taught me to push myself farther than I ever thought possible. I now know that when I reach a point in life when most people would just give up, I can continue to fight and push myself to my limit.

Sacrifice—In order to dance, I have had to sacrifice many things. The amount of sleep I get, my social life with school friends, my grades and being involved in multiple activities such as my school's musical or playing another sport are all

As a competition kid, I had a hard time understanding why so many choreographers were hard on me. Not until I was older did I realize that they were hard on me because they believed in me and liked my movement. They wanted to push me to make me stronger physically and mentally. I thank them for it now.

—Caroline Lewis
Professional Dancer, Choreographer, and Teacher

affected by my commitment to dance. But that is a decision I have made and I am OK with it. In fact, it is a true test of how far you are willing to go and how much you are willing to sacrifice in order to dance. Being able to prioritize your life is an important life skill.

Leadership—I started out at my current dance studio as the baby of the group. I was 12 years old dancing with dancers as old as 18 and 19. I learned so much from watching these older role models and now that I am the oldest, I can be a role model myself. Choose a studio where the teachers and choreographers are people you can look up to as well. Sometimes you are at the studio for more hours than your own home. Your teachers and fellow dancers become part of your family and you benefit from these relationships. Dancing with my role models has taught me how to be a leader.

Ideas for Careers in Dance and Using Your Dance Experience

I have met many people who love their work. Here are some ideas of things your can do and still be a part of dance when your are older.

Performer
- Broadway
- Videos
- Trade Shows/Corporate Shows

- Cruise Ships
- Theme Parks

Choreographer

Studio Owner

Dance Teacher/Faculty Member of University Dance Program

Producer or Director

Costume Designer

Make-up Artist

Dance Photographer

Professionals that Work with Dancers
- Physical Therapist
- Registered Dietitian
- Exercise Physiologist
- Fitness Instructor/Personal Trainer/Yoga/Pilates

Public Speaking and Presentations

Become a parent of a dancer

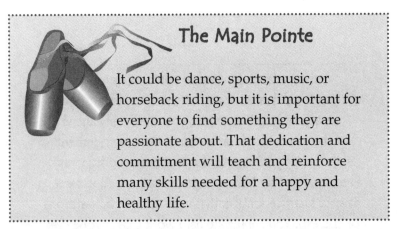

The Main Pointe

It could be dance, sports, music, or horseback riding, but it is important for everyone to find something they are passionate about. That dedication and commitment will teach and reinforce many skills needed for a happy and healthy life.

You are a leader! Whether your goal is to be a professional dancer or any other career, because you are a young, active dancer, you are already ahead of the game. You have excellent time management skills (don't you have to do your homework around rehearsals?). You have incredible discipline (don't you have to sacrifice social activities to attend competitions or classes?). You appreciate hard work (has anyone ever called you lazy?). So, the world out there is ready for you, and even if you don't know it right now, you are preparing for a successful career in any field that you choose! CONGRATS on your choice to dance. Enjoy every moment, every beat of it.

—Pam Chancey, Choreographer, Professional Dancer, Faculty for Broadway Dance Center and many other dance programs, producer of The Pulse Dance Convention

Recommended Resources

—with Jenna Lee Branner

The Care & Feeding of a Dancer resource list is available at:
www.thecareandfeedingof.us

Here you will find up-to-date lists of conventions, dance competitions, choreographers, equipment, books, magazines, Web site links, private coaches, and more.

This site also includes new recipes, training methods, and updates on any new research that would interest dancers.

Author Information

Toni Tickel Branner, MA

Exercise Physiologist, Wellness Consultant, Physical Educator, Professional Speaker

Professional Speaking, Workshops, and Seminars on Fitness, Nutrition and Stress Management

The Care & Feeding of a Dancer Studio Seminar for Parents and Students

The Care & Feeding of a Dancer Free E-Updates

The Care & Feeding of an Athlete Seminars for Parents and Athletes

The Care & Feeding of an Athlete Free E-Updates

The Care & Feeding of a Soccer Player On-the-field Seminar for Parents and Students

The Care & Feeding of a Soccer Player Free E-Updates

Health Made Simple Free E-Newsletter for people interested in general health, fitness and nutrition

Contact Toni at: Fitness Concepts

Web site: *www.tonibranner.com*
Email: *tonibranner@aol.com*
Phone: (704) 551-9051

Jenna Lee Branner: Student, Dancer, Singer, Model

Contact Jenna through *tonibranner@aol.com*

Books and Resources by Toni T. Branner, MA

The Care & Feeding of a Dancer by Toni T. Branner

The Care & Feeding of an Athlete by Toni T. Branner

The Care & Feeding of a Soccer Player by Toni T. Branner

Wilby's Fitness Book by Toni T. Branner

The Safe Exercise Handbook and Workout DVD with upper body and lower body exercise bands by Toni T. Branner (*www.tonibranner.com*)

Recommended Books for Athletes and Parents

Sports Success Rx! by Paul R. Stricker, MD

PowerPack for the Winning Edge
by Roy E. Vartabedian, PhD and Jack A. Medina, M.A.

The Right Moves: Preparing for Dance Competitions
by Pam Chancey

Dr. Sears' LEAN Kids
by William Sears, MD and Peter Sears, MD

The China Study by T. Colin Campbell

Prevent and Reverse Heart Disease
by Caldwell B. Esselstyn Jr., MD

Eat More, Weigh Less by Dean Ornish, MD

Hungry for Health by Susan Silberstein, PhD

The Omega-3 Connection by Andrew L. Stoll, MD

Digestive Tune-Up by John A. McDougall, MD

Dr. Neal Barnard's Program for Reversing Diabetes
by Neal D. Barnard, MD

Recommended Web sites and Newsletters

American Council on Exercise *(www.acefitness.org)*

American Heart Association *(www.americanheart.org)*

American Dietetic Association *(www.eatright.org)*

American College of Sports Medicine *(www.acsm.org)*

American College of Cardiology *(www.acc.org)*

American Cancer Society *(www.cancer.org)*

Fruit and Veggie Info and Recipes *(www.5aday.com)*

Center for Advancement in Cancer
Education *(www.beatcancer.org)*

Nutrition information unbiased by industry *(www.pcrm.org)*

The Wellness Forum *(www.wellnessforum.com)*

Dept. of Agriculture site for families
and children *(www.mypyramid.gov)*

Fruit and Veggie Info and Recipes *(www.vegweb.com)*

Bill Sears, MD Wellness Web site *(www.askdrsears.com)*

Product Recommendations

Fitness Equipment
For fairly priced, high quality fitness equipment, weights,
mats, stability balls, videos, etc.

Fitness Wholesale: 1-888-FW-ORDER or *fitnesswholesale.com*

For Juice Plus+˙ Whole Food Nutrition Products

Juice Plus+® provides the nutritional essence of 17 different
fruits, vegetables, and grains in convenient and inexpensive
capsule form.

For information and research
Go to: *www.juiceplus.com* or call 1-800-347-6350

(Children between 6 and 15 years are eligible to take
Juice Plus+®+® for free for up to three years as part of the
Children's Health Study if one adult takes the capsules.)

For Juice Plus+ Complete® Smoothie Mix
We recommend this product because it is plant-based protein
and is perfect for breakfast or for replacing glycogen in the
muscles after games or practice. High in calcium, Vitamin D,
phytonutrients and fiber.

Comes in French Vanilla, Dutch Chocolate, and Variety Pack

Go to: *www.juiceplus.com* or call 1-800-347-6350

**For Hundreds of Resources for Dancers or to sign up for
our free E-mail updates go to:**

www.thecareandfeedingof.us

Please contact us with feedback and comments on the material in this book. We would love to hear from you and visit your studio or hometown sometime. The best to you and your family and keep dancing!

—Sincerely, Toni and Jenna Branner

About the Authors

Toni Branner is director of Fitness Concepts, Inc., and teaches on topics such as anti-aging, children's wellness, motivation for lifestyle change, whole food nutrition, stress management and safe exercise.

Toni received her Master's Degree in Exercise Physiology from the University of North Carolina at Chapel Hill where she also served as director of the UNC Employee Health and Fitness Center and as a faculty member in the Department of Physical Education, Exercise and Sports Science.

Branner has authored two previous books. *The Safe Exercise Handbook* (5th Edition) promotes the importance of a regular exercise program as a means of improving your health and quality of life. This book is used on US Navy aircraft carriers to guide military personnel through their workouts. *Wilby's Fitness Book,* includes innovative ideas to help children stay healthy and feel good about themselves.

Through fitness classes for children and adults, as well as numerous speaking engagements, workshops and academic presentations, Toni has shown thousands of people the way to perform effective, injury-free fitness and achieve maximal health.

Jenna Branner is an award winning competitive dancer in Charlotte, NC. She has been dancing since she was three and competing since she was eight. Currently, Jenna competes with Weir Dancin' Inc., a nationally ranked dance studio, and dances there an average four to five hours a night, 3 to 4 nights a week after school. Her experience with dance has allowed her to learn life lessons of dedication, diligence, failure, and success which she wants to share with young dancers everywhere.

Jenna works with The Allegro Foundation, a non-profit organization that provides a dance/movement class for handicapped children and children with disabilities. She has won numerous scholarships and awards for her dancing and her work helping future dancers.